Creative Garden
Mosaics

Creative Garden
Mosaics

Dazzling Projects & Innovative Techniques

Jill MacKay

LARK BOOKS

A Division of Sterling Publishing Company, Inc.

New York

Editor
Terry Krautwurst

Art Director
Stacey Budge

Photographer
Evan Bracken

Photo Stylist
Susan McBride

Cover Designer
Barbara Zaretsky

Illustrators
Orrin Lundgren
Shannon Yokeley

Assistant Editors
Veronika Alice Gunter
Rain Newcomb
Heather Smith

Production Assistance
Lorelei Buckley
Shannon Yokeley

Editorial Assistance
Delores Gosnell

First Edition

Published by Lark Books, a division of
Sterling Publishing Co., Inc.
387 Park Avenue South, New York, N.Y. 10016

© 2003, Jill MacKay

Distributed in Canada by Sterling Publishing,
c/o Canadian Manda Group, One Atlantic Ave., Suite 105
Toronto, Ontario, Canada M6K 3E7

Distributed in the U.K. by Guild of Master Craftsman Publications Ltd.,
Castle Place, 166 High Street, Lewes, East Sussex, England
BN7 1XU
Tel: (+ 44) 1273 477374, Fax: (+ 44) 1273 478606, Email: pubs@thegmc-group.com, Web: www.gmcpublications.com

Distributed in Australia by Capricorn Link (Australia) Pty Ltd.,
P.O. Box 704, Windsor, NSW 2756 Australia

If you have questions or comments about this book, please contact:
Lark Books
67 Broadway
Asheville, NC 28801
(828) 253-0467
Manufactured in China

ISBN 1-57990-257-x

Table of Contents

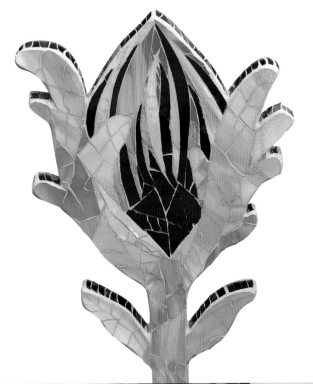

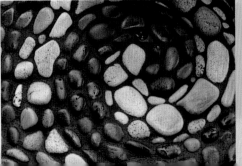

Introduction

The joke at my house is, if you stand still too long you'll find yourself covered in mosaic. Well, that's *a slight* exaggeration. But you really can add a lovely layer of mosaic to almost anything. Plus, you can create your own imaginative bases and other garden-art objects: planters, birdbaths, bed borders, and more. All you need are the right tools and materials, and a certain amount of know-how.

That, of course, is what this book is all about. But as you look through the pages, I hope you'll discover that this book is about something else, too: using your imagination and creativity to explore beyond the usual, the ordinary. You'll find very little traditional mosaic work here. Instead, the book focuses on nontraditional applications of materials, and the imaginative use and creation of objects to mosaic. My wish is that this book will open a door to new possibilities for you. It is intended as a starting point, one meant to spark new ideas.

I've tried to include a range of projects, from simple half-day endeavors to more advanced projects requiring greater skill and more time. Likewise, I've tried to introduce you to a range of styles, materials, and techniques, most of which are nontraditional and offer a wide freedom for the beginner.

Jill MacKay, *Pebble Mosaic Walkway* (opposite page, upper left), 1998-1999, 17 feet long (5.1 m). Photo by Evan Bracken.

Craigie, *Entrance Way* (opposite page, lower right), 2000, 1 x 5 feet (.3 x 1.5 m), glass on glass. Photo by Evan Bracken.

Craigie, *Untitled* (detail, opposite page, upper right and lower left), 1999, 7 x 3 feet (2.1 x .9 m), stained glass bar top. Photo by Evan Bracken.

Nina Ilitzky Solomon and Sue Chenoweth, *Forest Chair*, 2000, 37 ½ x 19 ½ x 17 inches (95.2 x 49.5 x 43.2 cm), handmade stoneware animal tiles and commercial porcelain tiles on cement-covered steel/styrofoam armature. Photo by James Cowlin.

Before you proceed any further, however, I feel compelled to warn you: This fascinating craft we call mosaic is addictive. Part of the attraction comes from the materials involved. Soon you'll find yourself amassing bits and pieces of things. The shattered remains of ordinary objects become useful leftovers that can be given new life as part of a mosaic pattern or design, embellishing the surface of another object. I've never been good at throwing anything away (it runs in the family; I get it from my father). The recycling aspect of mosaic suits my pack-rat nature, as it surely will yours. At the same time, there's nothing quite so exciting as the promise in a new sheet of stained glass, or in a box of tiles of a special color you've been wanting. Remember the feeling you had as a child when you opened a brand-new box of crayons?

Then too, there is the *process* of mosaic. Breaking and cutting things up and putting them back together again may sound tedious—even a little odd—but it's actually relaxing and rewarding. There is a special satisfaction that comes from creating beauty out of chaos, from making something old new again. As you

Jan Hinson, *Wingback Chair,* **1990,** 46 x 36 inches (117 x 91 cm), lightweight ferro-cement forms, reset broken tile. Photo by artist.

Cleo Mussi, *Three Wise Owls,* **1996,** 60 x 39 ½ x 19 ¾ inches (1.5 x 1 x .5 m), plywood and metal subframe, sauce pans, recycled and kiln-fired china. Photo by artist.

Cleo Mussi, *Platter Faces,* **2001,** 19 ¾ x 13 ¾ x ⁷/₁₆ inches (50 x 35 x 1 cm), recycled china. Photo by artist.

Mayor Baca's Art Summer Institute with Cassandra Reid, Mark Woody, and Daisy Kates, *Plants of New Mexico* **(detail), 2001,** 30 x 4 feet (9 x 1.2 m), handmade tile. Photo by Daisy Kates.

Lily Yeh and James "Big Man" Maxton, *Tree of Life,* **1995,** ceramic tile. Photo by Lily Yeh.

work on a mosaic you can see—and feel—your progress. The repeated gesture of gluing small fragments together to create a unified surface has a rhythm born from your own expression, and is just plain fun.

In an effort to get you started, I've tried my best to cover everything you'll need to know. In Chapter One we discuss tools, materials, and supplies. In Chapter Two you'll learn how to build a variety of bases—"mosaic-able" objects for the yard and garden used in several of the projects. In Chapter Three, we get down to the how-to of mosaicking itself: applying materials, tiling techniques, grouting, and more. And finally, in Chapter Four, you'll find detailed step-by-step instructions for more than 20 projects.

As you follow the instructions, don't be afraid to follow your own instincts too. For instance, I've included specific glass and tile colors in the materials lists for the projects. But I hope that after you've gained some experience you'll trust your own sense of color and let your own favorites reign. Likewise, I've provided color-keyed patterns, or templates, for many of the projects. Don't feel compelled to follow them exactly every time. Let your own sense of design shine through. And if a project comes out a little different (or even a lot different) from the one shown in the book, great! There's nothing wrong with that; in fact, celebrate the difference. Make the projects your own. Take risks and make mistakes—that's the best way to learn and discover.

Being a creative individual, expressing yourself through creating (a friend of mine calls it being a "maker") is one of the greatest joys in life. My hope is that this book will encourage you to try new things, to stretch your limits and abilities a little further, while you make some wonderful mosaics for your yard and garden.

Enjoy!

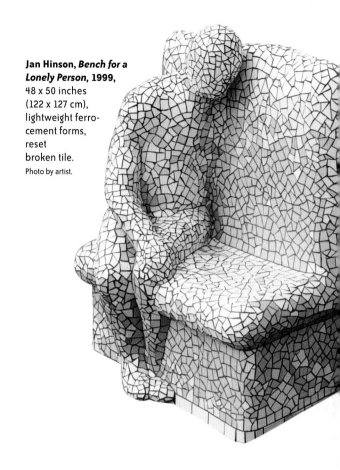

Jan Hinson, *Bench for a Lonely Person*, 1999, 48 x 50 inches (122 x 127 cm), lightweight ferro-cement forms, reset broken tile. Photo by artist.

Nina Ilitzky Solomon, *City Mural* (for The Tucson Museum of Art: Education Courtyard Renovation Project), 2001, 48 x 60 x 1 inches (1.2 x 1.5 m x 2.5 cm), handmade tiles, pebbles, cement board panels, grout. Photo by Dan Soloman.

CHAPTER ONE

Getting Started

Craigie, *Untitled*, 2001,
18 x 4 inches (45.7 x 10 cm), stone glass on wood.
Photo by Evan Bracken.

Materials

Here's another great reason for learning how to mosaic: You don't have to invest a lot of money to get started. Just a few basic materials and supplies will do.

TESSERAE

All sorts of different materials can be used as *tesserae,* the mosaicist's term for the bits of this and pieces of that used together in a mosaic. In fact, much of the fun of mosaic work is in discovering the possibilities offered by materials old and new. Once you start thinking like a mosaicist, you find yourself looking at things like broken dishes and stray pebbles in a whole different way. Collecting glass, tile, stone, bits of china, and more becomes a favorite pastime.

The materials listed here represent only a partial sampling of the possibilities for use in making mosaics.

Vitreous Glass Tile

Widely available and popular with mosaicists, vitreous glass tiles are manufactured in several sizes but the standard is ¾ inch (1.9 cm) square, with ⅜-inch (9.5 mm) square "mini" tiles now gaining popularity, too. The tiles are about ⅛ inch (3 mm) thick and have a smooth, flat upper surface. Most are grooved on the underside and have a beveled edge, to improve adhesion. Because they're vitreous— in other words, nonporous—the tiles are stain-resistant and frost-proof, making them ideal for out-door projects. What's more, they're relatively easy to cut into circles, smaller squares, and other shapes.

Best of all, vitreous glass tiles are available in an amazing range of colors, from pale pastels to bold, vibrant hues. Among my favorites are the metallic colors, which have sparkling, coppery veins running through them.

Vitreous glass tiles are machine-made, unlike the handmade mosaic glass squares known as *smalti,* which are produced in Italy using centuries-old methods. Also unlike smalti, however, vitreous glass tiles are relatively inexpensive. Crafts stores sell small bags of tiles, or you can buy loose tiles from some sup-pliers by the pound—a more eco-nomical approach. In most cases there are about 140 to 160 tiles per pound (454 g).

You'll also find a variety of specialty vitreous glass tiles on the market—unique, artist-crafted tiles made of fused glass.

Stained Glass

Fortunately, there's no reason to limit yourself to materials precut into squares or other shapes specifically for mosaic work. You can easily cut your own tiles for tesserae (see page 19), which opens up a much wider world of possibilities—including one of my favorites, stained glass.

Stained glass is available in almost any color and color combination imaginable, and adds a look of richness not obtainable with other materials. There are single-color glasses, both transparent and opaque. There are multi-colored glasses, some with swirls of inter-mixed colors (which we refer to in this book as "mix" stained glass) and some with ringlike patterns ("mottled" stained glass).

What's more, there are many stained glasses with special surface effects. Opalescent stained glass, made with a white base to which other colors are added, is highly reflective, producing a beautiful, luminescent glow. Iridescent or iridized stained glass has thin layers of metallic crystal bonded to its surface, creating a shimmering shifting of multiple colors similar to what you see when you look at a drop of oil in a puddle. The effect varies with the base color—dark iridized glass has a reflective quality entirely different from light or pastel iridized glass—but all are beautiful and magical.

Stained glass (as well as mirror and clear glass) is most commonly sold in 12 x 12-inch (30.5 x 30.5 cm) sheets. When you're first

Clockwise from left: silver and colored mirror, "mix" stained glass, "mottled" stained glass, clear and textured glass

starting out you'll probably have to buy glass by the sheet for mosaic projects—but as your experience grows, so will your supply of scraps. Note that when I list materials for the projects in this book I specify a "sheet" only when you'll need that much. Otherwise I specify a "piece" of a certain size, so that you can utilize scraps as much as possible. One more tip: If there are stained-glass artists in your area, introduce yourself; they're usually thrilled to pass along scrap pieces they don't need.

Mirror

When used properly, mirror can bring a sparkle of life to a mosaic like nothing else. This is because mirror is always reflecting the conditions and objects surrounding it. The changing light of day, the varying colors of light, the shifting seasons—they're reflected in the mirror, giving your work an ever-changing quality. An outdoor mosaic containing a proportionate amount of mirror seems to come alive, like the

natural setting around it.

Be aware, however, that it's easy to overdo mirror when using it in mosaics—especially in the case of ordinary silver mirror. Colored mirror is subtler, and is therefore easier to incorporate into projects. It can reflect and complement the colors of glass or tile it's placed next to. Using mirror as an outline on a piece, or to tile the edge, is effective because its reflective quality highlights, rather than overpowers, the other materials.

Mirror comes in a wide variety of colors. The only color I have never seen (but would like to) is a true red. Colored mirror and plain silver mirror are available at stained glass stores and on the Internet.

Textured and Clear Glass

Clear glass comes in a variety of surface textures—rippled, hammered, stippled, and more. The textures can add a decorative quality to a mosaic, in much the way wallpaper spices up a room, but with the translucency only glass can provide.

Plain, untextured clear glass also can be useful and quite striking. Not every mosaic, after all, is designed to cover up a surface. Sometimes the objective is simply to add dimension—which clear glass does nicely. For example, in some projects (such as the Multi-Faceted Gazing Face on page 116 and the Pillar Planter Under Glass on page 95) I paint the base, and then apply tesserae I've cut from double-thickness clear glass to add depth and sparkle.

Clear glass tesserae applied over a painted surface add depth, and highlight the base and grout colors.

Make Your Own Gold Leaf Glass

Authentic gold-leaf tesserae, in which gold leaf is sandwiched between layers of glass, are exceedingly expensive. Use this technique to produce composite gold-leaf glass for a fraction of the cost, and then cut it as needed into shards or tesserae.

MATERIALS

· Composite gold leaf and adhesive
· Double-thickness clear glass

1 Following the manufacturer's instructions, brush a coat of gold-leaf adhesive onto the glass. The glass should be as big as or slightly smaller than a sheet of gold leaf, typically 5 inches (12.7 cm) square.

2 Let the adhesive dry clear. Then carefully lay a sheet of gold leaf onto the glass. Because gold leaf is feather-light and less than paper thin, it can be difficult to handle and position. Just get as much on the glass as possible.

3 Smooth the gold leaf carefully over the surface.

4 Trim excess gold leaf from the edges and smooth it onto remaining clear areas.

5 Cut the glass gold-leaf-side up (to minimize scratching the gold leaf) into shards. Or follow the instructions on page 19 for making square and rectangular tiles.

I also use double-thickness clear glass to make an affordable substitute for the world's most expensive mosaic material: hand-made gold-leaf tesserae. Authentic gold-leaf tesserae are made by sandwiching gold leaf between fused layers of glass. They're strikingly beautiful. The cost, however, makes genuine gold-leaf tesserae impractical for many projects.

After a little experimenting I came up with what I think is a good alternative. I apply inexpensive composite gold leaf, which is sold along with a special adhesive in crafts stores, to double-thickness clear glass. Then I cut the glass into squares or shards for tesserae. It looks great. The only disadvantage is that the gold leaf can scratch easily—so before I use the tesserae, I paint the surface I'll be mosaicking with metallic gold enamel to help hide any scratches. To try this technique, follow the instructions in Make Your Own Gold Leaf Glass (left).

Ceramic Tile

There are dozens of kinds of ceramic tiles: glazed and unglazed, shiny and matte finish, big—as in 4 x 4-inch (10.2 x 10.2 cm)—and small, as in little ⅜-inch (9.5 mm) squares. The larger sizes can be broken into pieces and used as tesserae; the smaller tiles can be used as-is or cut and nipped into varying shapes. For our purposes, the most important consideration is whether the tile will stand up to weather, and particularly to the freeze-thaw

cycle typical of many climates. In general, ordinary ceramic wall tiles are *not* suitable for outdoor mosaics. Such tiles are porous and absorb water that can then freeze, causing cracking.

Some ceramic tile has been high-fired and is designated "frostproof" or "frost resistant." Floor tiles are often rated specifically for water absorption. "Vitrified" floor tiles have an absorption rating between 0.5 and 3 percent, and can withstand freeze-thaw cycles. Porcelain floor tiles have an even lower absorption rating, but come in a limited range of colors.

Most ceramic tile made specifically for mosaic use is frostproof. Among them are tiles that aren't glazed at all; the color is mixed right into the clay. They come in a nice range of colors and are extremely durable, making them a good choice for outdoor projects.

You can also buy small ceramic tiles in a variety of specialty shapes—hearts, triangles, leaves, and more.

China

Making mosaics from broken dishes—china and dinnerware—is a technique known as *pique assiette*, which translated literally from the French means "plate scrounger." The bright colors and patterns in castoff china and dinnerware can add wonderful interest and contrast to a contemporary mosaic. Again, however, it's important to make sure the material is frost-proof. High-fired dinnerware and porcelain are best.

Pebbles, Stones, and Agates

The first and oldest mosaics were made using pebbles, and for good reason. They offer an infinite variety of shapes and colors. From a mosaicist's point of view, the ideal pebble has a consistent shape with at least one flat side and has been worn smooth by tumbling in an ocean or stream. Most of us will never walk enough beaches to gather a good collection and selection of pebbles. Luckily you can buy them by the pound, polished and unpolished, in craft stores and nurseries.

A wide variety of materials can be used as tesserae, including (clockwise from left) agate slices, glass globs, ceramic tiles and specialty shapes, pebbles, seashells, jewels, and vitreous glass tiles.

Polished agate slices can be used as focal points in a design or to contrast with other materials such as stained glass. Available in rock and hobby shops, agate slices are quite spectacular in their shape and pattern as well as color. Of course, the Internet is also a good source for these natural materials.

Other Tesserae

Found objects, seashells, cut crystal, glass globs and beads, synthetic jewels—almost anything goes in mosaic. Best of all, because of the Internet, almost any material is available to you. Many sites specialize in selling mosaic materials. Internet auction sites also are excellent sources.

Craigie, *Gecko*, 2000, 4 x 5 feet x 8 inches (1.2 x 1.5 m x 20.3 cm), stained glass. Photo by Evan Bracken.

ADHESIVES

Obviously, when you're making mosaics intended for the outdoors it's important to choose the right adhesive. The adhesive must be waterproof, weather-resistant, and suited to the surface material. Always remember when working with any solvent-based glues to provide proper ventilation.

Cement-Based Tile Adhesive

Otherwise known as thin-set mortar, cement-based tile adhesive is generally recommended for adhering tesserae, and particularly ceramic materials, to cement board and other cement-based surfaces. Mortar is a combination of sand, Portland cement, and water. The types of mortars used for mosaics and tile installations are called "thin-set" because they're much thinner than mortars used for laying cement block and bricks. Look for "polymer-fortified" thin-set tile adhesive, which contains polymer additives that

improve the mortar's strength and durability. Different brands require different mixing procedures, so be sure to follow the manufacturer's instructions. Pay attention, as well, to temperature requirements; many cement-based adhesives cannot be applied below certain temperatures.

Silicone Glues

These are my favorite adhesives; I use silicone glue for bonding tesserae to most surface types, including wood, polymer clay, ceramics—and even fiber cement and cement board, especially when the tesserae are glass rather than ceramic. Silicone glues have great holding power, which makes them particularly good when working on vertical surfaces. Also called silicone sealant, the adhesives are sold in caulking-gun cartridges. I prefer the smaller tubes, however, which are easier to use and more appropriate for all but the largest projects. You can squeeze the glue directly onto

the surface and then use a craft stick to spread it around. I use clear silicone rather than opaque for most projects because the clear is invisible and doesn't detract from the beauty of the glass or other materials.

Choose a silicone adhesive that's rated for exterior use; it should be waterproof and frost-proof. Always read the information on the label and follow the manufacturer's instructions.

Multipurpose Waterproof Glues

These are sold in tubes and bottles and are also good for most surface types, except those that are cement-based. I use them mostly when the base object and the tesserae are very small, which makes spreading silicone difficult. Don't mistake these glues for common hobby-type PVA (polyvinyl acetate) "white glue," which is not waterproof and is suitable only for indoor use. Read the label and make sure the glue is weather-resistant.

GROUT

Grout is the cement-based material used to fill the spaces between tesserae. More than just a filler, though, grout physically strengthens the work by cementing it together. It surrounds all the pieces and unites them. Grout also can be a major design element. Grout lines can emphasize the flow or shape of an object and its design features, or they can move in random directions. Grout color, especially, can have a strong influence on the appearance of a finished piece. Bright grout colors add energy and give a mosaic a busy, fractured feel. Neutral colors and those closest in hue to the tesserae draw a mosaic's elements together, creating a more unified appearance.

There are two basic kinds of grout: unsanded and sanded. The standard rule for choosing between the two is to use sanded grout when the space between tiles is wider than $\frac{1}{8}$ inch (3 mm), and unsanded when the width is less. If you use unsanded grout in a wide space, it'll crack. In my work I use only sanded grout, no matter what the project. I prefer its consistency; it has a better sculptural quality than unsanded grout. Also, the sand helps you to clean and polish the surface after grouting; it acts like a little built-in buffer as you wipe the glass with cloth.

I do something else that goes against standard grout procedure: I don't use any water when I mix my grout. Most mosaicists mix their grout with water, and then stir in an acrylic grout fortifier to increase the grout's strength and durability. I use fortifier for all the liquid. This makes the grout more flexible and easier to work with, and also provides extra protection from the elements outdoors.

Grouts and grout fortifier (also sometimes called acrylic mortar additive or admix) are sold in home improvement and building supply centers. Grout is available in white and in a variety of colors. However, the color choices are not always just right for a particular project. To solve that problem, you can custom color your grout when you mix it. There are various coloring agents you can use for this purpose, including acrylic art paints and powdered pigments. In my opinion, though, the best choice is liquid pure pigment, concentrated colorants sold in art supply stores in 2-ounce (60 mL) bottles. Many of the projects in this book specify custom grout colors, produced either by starting with white grout and adding all the color as liquid pigment(photos upper left), or by starting with a colored grout and adding pigment to change the hue. Yellow pigment added to blue grout, for instance, yields green.

Tools

Most mosaic studios are equipped with the same basic tools, plus a few specialty tools of one sort or another, depending on the artist's particular interests, material preferences, and style. If you're a beginner, you don't have to go out and buy every tool in the book right away. Start with simple projects and the tools needed for them. Make sure, though, that the tools you do buy are good ones. Always get the best you can afford.

CUTTING TOOLS

Glasscutter

I use my glasscutter for making square or rectangular tesserae from stained glass and mirror, for slicing large sheets of glass into more manageable sizes, for cutting strips of glass for tiling edges, and for gradual curving cuts, such as when I'm creating a simple leaf shape (see page 45). The tool has a small metal wheel at one end for scoring glass, and a metal ball at the other end for tapping the glass to encourage a break along the score line. Glasscutters range from basic models with steel wheels to more elaborate (and more expensive) models with replaceable carbide wheels and refillable oil reservoirs in the handle. The reservoir releases a small amount of oil to the cutter wheel and glass, making the cut somewhat easier and keeping the wheel sharp. When using a glasscutter, push it forward with just enough downward pressure to score the surface—the cutting wheel makes a distinct scratching sound against the glass when you're doing it right.

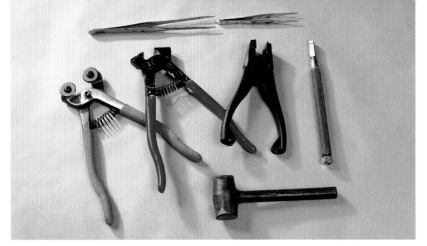

Basic mosaic tools: (top) tweezers; (center, left to right) glass mosaic cutters, ceramic tile nippers, running pliers, glasscutter; (bottom) hammer

Running Pliers

This tool is a companion to a glasscutter and is used to break glass neatly along a score line. Running pliers are made from lightweight, high-strength plastic. They have a small white line on the outside of the upper jaw that corresponds with a raised ridge on the inside of the lower jaw. After scoring a piece of glass with a glasscutter, grasp the glass at one edge with running pliers, with the white mark on the pliers aligned directly over the score line, and gently squeeze. The pressure and leverage pushes the glass down over the raised ridge, causing the break to "run" up the score line, separating the pieces cleanly.

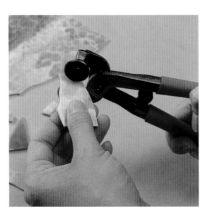

Glass mosaic cutters

Glass Mosaic Cutters

This tool, also sometimes called a wheeled glass nipper, has handles like pliers and two carbide cutting wheels instead of jaws. The handles are sprung, so the jaws are always open until you squeeze the handles, which brings the wheels together. One hand holds the glass while the other cuts with gentle scissor-like pressure. I use glass mosaic cutters more than any other tool for cutting and shaping stained glass, mirror, and vitreous glass tiles. The tool cuts small curves as well as straight lines, so it's an enormous help for shaping pieces with complicated contours, and for creating irregular shards (photo lower left). You can also use glass mosaic cutters to nip vitreous glass tiles into all sorts of shapes, including squares, triangles, crescents, and circles.

Some glass mosaic cutters have wheels that rotate freely, while other models have wheels that can be tightened in a stationary position. I recommend the stationary type; there's less slippage when cutting, so you have more control. When the wheels' cutting edges become dull you can loosen the wheels, turn them slightly, and tighten them back up, giving you a sharp new cutting edge. The wheels on both types of cutters are replaceable.

Hammer

Obviously it's not a precision cutting tool, but a hammer is invaluable when working with ceramic tile. There's no better way to break up large tile, such as a standard 4 x 4-inch (10.2 x 10.2 cm) tile, into pieces for tesserae. Put on a leather glove, place the tile face down in your gloved hand, and strike the center of the tile's back side (photo lower right). The tile will break into three or four pieces. The larger pieces can then be struck again to create smaller pieces, or you can cut them using tile nippers. Don't use this method if you have carpal tunnel syndrome, because your hand and wrist absorb the shock of the strike. Instead, put the tile face down on a thick cloth or towel and strike it with a hammer.

A hammer is the perfect tool for breaking ceramic tile into smaller pieces.

Ceramic tile nippers

Ceramic Tile Nippers

This tool has handles like pliers and is designed to give you maximum leverage, so they do most of the tile-cutting work, not you. Like glass mosaic cutters, they have spring-action handles so they don't have to be pulled apart every time you cut. The jaws of good nippers are made of tungsten carbide so they're durable, though over time they can still become dulled. Nippers are good for cutting ceramic tile and crockery into smaller pieces (photo above), and can also be used for cutting and shaping vitreous glass tiles.

When using ceramic tile nippers place the jaws so that they overlap the tile's edge by no more than $1/8$ to $1/4$ inch (3 to 6 mm). Line up the jaws so they point in the direction of the cut you want to make, then squeeze the handles firmly. A good pair of nippers is a must; prices vary according to quality.

Tile-Making Kit

Glasscutter
Running pliers
Ruler
Safety goggles

Making Tiles From Glass and Mirror

When vitreous glass tiles don't offer the color or look you want, you can cut your own square or rectangular tiles from stained glass or mirror. Cut them to whatever size you wish. Use them as they are, or nip and shape them just as you would storebought tiles.

1 Determine the width of the tile you wish to cut. Place a ruler at that width along one edge of the glass and use the glasscutter to score along that line.

2 Make additional score lines parallel to the first, spaced to match the first strip's width. Using running pliers, snap off the entire scored section at the last score line. Then turn the scored section and with the glasscutter cut a second set of score lines perpendicular to the first set, creating a grid, as shown in the photo.

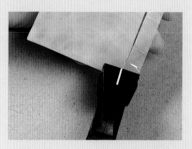

3 Align the running pliers with the first lengthwise score line you made and snap off the first strip. Then snap off the rest of the long strips.

4 Turn each strip and use running pliers along the second set of score lines to snap off individual tiles one at a time.

Ceramic tile cutter

Ceramic Tile Cutter

This is a tabletop tool designed primarily for cutting ceramic tile for wall and floor installations (photo above). But it's also great for mosaics when you need to cut ceramic tile into straight sections of a given width—for tiling edges, for example. The tool consists of a tungsten carbide wheel that scores the tile. Behind the scoring wheel is a gripper/snapper that snaps the tile on the score line. Both are connected to a long handle that moves along a track. Set the cutter's adjustable ruled edges to the desired width, position the tile on the cutting track, and push the handle forward to score the tile. Then position the gripper/snapper over the score and push down on the handle to separate the pieces. Some tile cutters also can make diagonal cuts. There's a pliers-like handheld version of this tool, also called a ceramic tile cutter, but I prefer the tabletop model; it's easier to use.

Ring Saw

A ring saw is a specialty power wet saw marketed to stained glass artists. It has a circular wire blade encrusted with diamond burs; the blade is surrounded by water inside a reservoir. The ring saw allows cutting in any direction, which gives you great control and freedom of expression—you can cut virtually any shape. You can use a heavy blade for cutting ceramic tile or a lighter blade for stained glass. The saw will also cut plastics and metal—but not fingers, so it's safe even for children. Ring saws are expensive, so investing in one makes sense only if you'll use it often. If you only occasionally need glass or mirror cut to a complex shape, take the job to a stained glass or glass shop in your area that has a ring saw.

OTHER TOOLS

Craft Sticks

Wooden craft sticks—like the stick handles on frozen ice cream treats—are a must for spreading adhesive on a section of a project before tiling or for "buttering" tesserae—the term for spreading adhesive on individual tesserae before placing them. You'll want lots of craft sticks on hand because adhesive builds up on them quickly and you need to change to a fresh stick often to keep your work from getting messy. Craft sticks also are useful for cleaning excess adhesive and grout from pebbles, which other tools can scratch.

Trowels and Squeegees

When spreading cement-based adhesives on large flat areas, use a flat bed trowel; avoid notched trowels because there's a risk of moisture buildup in the furrows they create. A small pointing trowel is useful for getting adhesive into tight, awkward spots. For really large projects, spread cement-based adhesives with a flat-bladed squeegee.

Tweezers

At least one pair of long craft tweezers is a must for manipulating, positioning, and placing tesserae too small to manage with your fingers. Use whatever size is most comfortable for you.

Grouting Sponge

Any sponge will do for wiping excess grout off a freshly grouted project. A grouting sponge, however, does double duty because it has two surfaces. One side is like a regular sponge for wiping; the other side has a soft but abrasive surface good for buffing and polishing glass and tile without scratching it. Alternatively, you can use a soft cloth for polishing.

Cleaning Tools

Dental tools, craft sticks, hobby knife blades and single-edge razor blades are the tools of choice for removing bits of dried adhesive before grouting and for cleaning away dried grout residue. Dental picks in various sizes are particularly good for getting into nooks and crannies. When you go to the dentist, ask if they have any tools headed for the trash. I've also found dental tools at flea markets. Another kind of dental tool— a kid-size toothbrush—is perfect for cleaning grout from vitreous glass tiles, which have a surface that tends to hold grout residue. I wet the toothbrush and scrub the tiles one at a time.

Lazy Susan

A lazy Susan, rotating TV base, or some other type of flat turntable will make your life easier for most projects. It gives you access to all sides of an object, enabling you to turn, view and work on it from any angle without having to lift or move the object itself. Moving a piece before adhesive or grout has fully dried is always a risk.

GENERAL SUPPLIES

Containers

Mixing bowls, buckets, plastic tubs—collect them all, in whatever sizes you find, so you'll have a selection on hand for mixing varying quantities of grout, fiber cement, and other materials. When my collection of recycled containers doesn't offer what I need for projects, I buy inexpensive plastic buckets sold in various sizes in paint and building supply stores.

Plastic Sheeting

You'll need plastic for covering your work surface and for wrapping projects to allow fiber cement and grout to cure. I keep heavyweight plastic sheeting on my work surface all the time, and put an additional layer down just before grouting or using fiber cement. Then I don't have to strip the whole table when I'm finished. I remove just the extra piece, which often can be saved for another time. Cut-open plastic trash bags are an acceptable substitute when you don't have plastic sheeting.

Kraft Paper

Paper or plastic? If you prefer, you can use plain brown kraft paper instead of plastic for covering your work surface and for wrapping projects during curing. Kraft paper is sold inexpensively in rolls in building supply stores.

Masking Tape

A supply of masking tape in various widths is a must for securing wrapped projects, for taping off parts of projects before grouting, and for all-around use.

Miscellaneous

This includes all the other "stuff" you'll accumulate naturally in your work area over time: rags and brushes for general cleaning, jars and bins for storing various materials, paper plates for holding tesserae, etc.

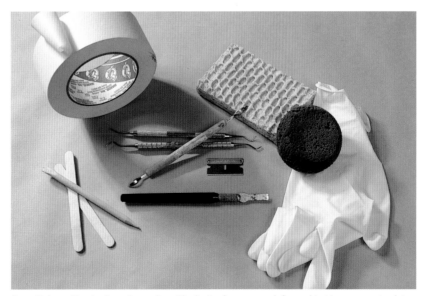

Essential grouting tools and supplies. Clockwise from upper left: masking tape, sponges, latex gloves, cleaning tools, clay modeling tools, craft sticks.

Basic Mosaic Supply Kit

A list of the basic supplies you'll need for virtually every project in this book:

Plastic for covering
   work surface
Paper plates for holding
   tesserae
Craft sticks
Tweezers
Containers for mixing grout
Container for water
Sponge
Polishing cloth
Razor blades
Cleaning tools
   (dental picks, etc.)
Plastic or kraft paper for
   wrapping object
Latex gloves
Safety goggles
Dust mask

SAFETY FIRST!

Never scrimp or take shortcuts when it comes to safety. Always protect your health; it's precious.

Safety Equipment

Safety goggles are a must when operating power tools and cutting any material, especially glass and tile. Small particles and splinters fly when cutting and nipping. I also wear goggles whenever I'm mixing dry materials, such as fiber cement or grout, to protect my eyes from the dust. Store goggles in a sealed plastic bag when not in use to keep them clean.

A quality dust mask also is essential. Be conscientious about wearing it every time you do anything that creates airborne particles, which includes cutting and breaking tiles. When working with cementitious materials (mixing grout, fiber cement, etc.), inhaling the dust can cause serious damage to your lungs and sinuses over time. Keep your mask in a sealed plastic bag when not in use so dust won't build up on it, defeating its purpose.

Always wear latex or rubber gloves when mixing or using grout or fiber cement. I prefer latex gloves because they fit like a second skin. They're also more economical, especially when purchased by the box. I often wear two pairs, because fingertips tend to break through the ends. It's also a good idea to wear latex gloves when using silicone glue for tiling; the gloves help keep your hands clean. Plus, if your fingers get too goopy with glue midway through a project, you can just slip off the gluey gloves and put on a new pair.

Cleaning Up

Make a habit of cleaning up after every work session. Bits of glass, tile, and other materials accumulate quickly. Wear protective gear when sweeping the floor and counters. Glass can break down into particles tiny enough to become airborne when swept.

Never rinse grout or cement down your drains. These materials will set up, or harden, underwater, damaging your pipes in a big way. Instead, use a "slop" container—a large bucket or plastic garbage pail filled with water—to collect cement residue for disposal. Submerge and rinse off grout and cement mixing containers in the slop bucket. Rinse your hands and tools in a separate bucket filled with clean water, then empty that bucket into the slop container. To clean out the slop container, let the contents settle overnight, then pour off the water and dump the sludge at the bottom into a plastic garbage bag for disposal.

Wash and dry your tools. Spray metal tools with a protective lubricant so they won't rust. I use pump-action spray cooking oil on my metal tools.

Work Area Precautions

Never let others come near you while you're cutting or nipping unless they're wearing eye protection, too.

Don't put food or an open drink near you when you're working with glass or tile. Otherwise you'll end up eating or drinking tiny splinters.

Keep children and pets out of your work area. You can make an exception with children if you're willing to supervise them closely and if they put shoes on, but pets' paws can't be protected.

Always keep your work area well-ventilated, especially when working with polymer clay and solvent-based adhesives.

CHAPTER TWO

Building Bases and Armatures

You can mosaic just about any solid surface, which of course leaves the door wide open to possibilities. Almost any existing object is fair game. In this book alone, there are projects for mosaicking a wall, tabletop, lantern, brick, porcelain frog, flowerpots, and rocks.

But you can also create your own bases, or objects to mosaic. One way is to add onto an existing item, and then mosaic the entire "improved" base, as in the Sugar-and-Cream Strawberry Planter project—with added teacups—on page 86. Or you can simply build from scratch, fashioning any of a variety of materials into the objects you want.

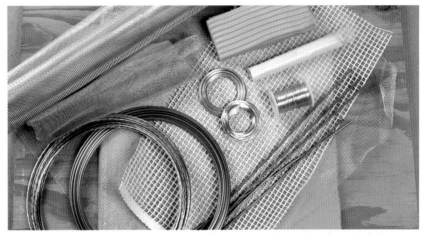

Armature and base-building materials: (stacked, from bottom up) wood, reinforced cement board, form-holding woven wire mesh, cotton latch-hook mesh, wire window screen; (left to right), steel cable wire, armature wire, steel rod, thin-gauge flexible wire, polymer modeling compound, epoxy putty

Armature-Building Materials and Tools

Sometimes building a base involves first creating an *armature,* which is the internal structure that gives form to and supports sculptures and other formed bases. Armatures generally consist of two parts: a rigid skeleton that provides structural strength and holds the sculpture together, and a flexible "skin," such as wire screening, that provides contour and supports a covering material such as fiber cement or epoxy.

Depending on the project, materials for the skeleton can be anything from steel cable or wire to polystyrene or PVC pipe. I've made armatures from various found materials, too, such as a leftover piece of flexible metal tubing used for ventilating clothes dryers. Regardless, an armature must be capable of supporting itself and everything you'll add to it, including the surface coating and the mosaic tesserae and grout. It should be self-supporting or fastened to or embedded in something stable.

Watch the Weather

Be sure to use objects and materials that will withstand the weather, particularly freeze-thaw cycles. Ordinary terra cotta, for example, is porous and cracks in a freeze-thaw climate. But a high-fired ceramic pot won't. If your seasonal temperatures regularly dip below freezing, use only frost-hardy materials—or bring frost-susceptible projects indoors when the weather turns cold.

Bruce & Shannon Kelly Andersen, *Aqua,*
2001, 41 x 41 x 21 inches (1 m x 1 m x
53.3 cm), steel, concrete, stoneware
mosaic tile. Photo by Bruce Andersen.

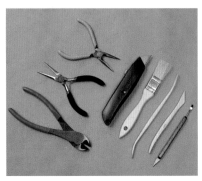

Armature and base-building tools clockwise
from lower left: wire cutters, needle-nose
pliers, heavy-duty utility knife, slurry brush,
clay modeling tools, clay cleanup tool

Steel rasps are helpful for smoothing
and developing detail when working
with fiber cement.

WIRE AND METAL MESH

Perhaps most often I use wire and
metal mesh for building armatures. The materials are flexible,
strong, and can be adapted to a
wide range of projects. Ordinary
steel cable, wire, metal lath, hard-
ware cloth, window screening, and
chicken wire all can be useful.

In addition, art supply stores
sell wire and metal mesh made
specifically for creating armatures.
These materials are exceptionally
easy to use and won't rust or
create stains. Armature wire is
sold in various gauges, both with
and without plastic covering.
Usually made of aluminum, it's
extremely pliable so you can bend
it into almost any shape. Form-
holding woven wire mesh, also
called modeler's mesh or sculptor's
mesh, is available in various
weaves, from a fine fabric-like
material to more open square
and diamond-shaped meshes.
You can bend, stretch, and
mold it over structural skeletons
to create complex contours
and shapes.

Wire and metal mesh also can
be used to create armatures for
extensions or additions to bases.
Metal mesh is ideal for making
curving structures, such as the
arch for the Garden Shrine
project (page 100). Needle-nose
pliers, wire cutters, and scissors
or metal-cutting shears are all
you'll need for working with most
wire and metal mesh.

Base-Building Materials and Tools

In mosaic terms, a "base" is any
object to which you apply tesserae.
By making your own bases, you
give yourself the creative freedom
to mosaic almost anything.

FIBER CEMENT AND SLURRY

Fiber cement is a mixture of
Portland cement and acrylic
fortifier with steel-wool fibers
added for extra strength. When
made properly it has the feel and
sculptural qualities of clay. Applied
over an armature or base, it hardens into a solid and durable surface
that can then be mosaicked.

Slurry is a binder, a mixture of
Portland cement and fortifier with
a consistency similar to house
paint. Before applying fiber
cement, always brush on a coating
of slurry to wet the surface and
give the fiber cement something
to bond to. If a slurried area dries
before you can apply cement, brush
it with slurry again, and then add
the fiber cement. Likewise, slurry
an existing layer of fiber cement
before adding another layer.

Mix just one batch of fiber
cement at a time, because if you
mix too much at once it'll set
up before you can use it all.
The recipe on page 25 makes
enough for an initial layer for
most projects. Use your fingers
to press and smooth on the
material. The smoother the
surface, the easier it will be to tile.

Your hands are your most
important tools when working with
fiber cement—just be sure always to

wear gloves to protect them from cement's caustic nature. Use a potter's rib—or a homemade version, a 3 x 4-inch (7.6 x 10.2 cm) piece of plastic cut from a milk jug—to evenly smooth wet fiber cement. Clay modeling tools are helpful for sculpting details. When the cement is nearly set up but still somewhat damp, use steel rasps to file away any lumps and bumps. You'll also need a small wire brush to remove buildup in the rasps' teeth as you work, and to clean them when finished.

Like grout and any other cement-based product, fiber cement must slowly cure, or go through the chemical process known as *hydration,* in order to attain maximum hardness. Cement or concrete left to dry in the open air loses moisture too quickly and will reach only 30 to 40 percent of its potential hardness. Wrap any freshly fiber-cemented work in plastic and keep it in a cool place for three to five days before tiling or otherwise working on it.

Fiber Cement Supply Kit

Container or cup for slurry
Brush for slurry
Bucket or other container
    for fiber cement
Potter's rib or 3 x 4-inch
    (7.6 x 10.2 cm) rectangle cut
    from plastic milk jug
Latex gloves
Dust mask
Safety goggles

Basic Fiber Cement

16 ounces (480 mL) of acrylic
    grout fortifier
½ biscuit of medium fine
    (#0 or #1) steel wool
3 ¼ pounds (1.5 kg) of white
    or gray Portland cement

1 Pull apart the steel wool to loosen and separate the fibers. Using scissors, snip the steel wool into the container in small bits.

2 Add the acrylic grout fortifier.

3 Add Portland cement, about 8 ounces (240 mL) at a time, mixing thoroughly after each addition. Be sure to wear gloves, dust mask, and goggles.

4 When completely mixed, the fiber cement should be smooth and have the consistency of wet clay.

Basic Slurry

2 parts white or gray Portland
    cement
1 part acrylic grout fortifier

Mix the slurry thoroughly in a container. I usually make between 1 and 2 cups (240 to 480 mL) at a time. Use an inexpensive brush to apply the slurry.

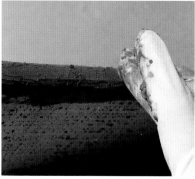

To level a rough edge on cut cement board, brush the edge with slurry, then smooth on a layer of fiber cement.

WOOD

Because it's easy to cut, wood is a logical choice for bases that involve curving or complex contours, such as the garden stake on page 58. Be sure to choose rot-resistant wood—either exterior- or marine-grade plywood, or a naturally resistant wood such as cedar. To minimize the possibility of warping, use wood at least ¾ inch (1.9 cm) thick.

To further reduce the chances of damage from rotting and warping, brush two coats of outdoor wood sealer onto the wood—including the edges— before tiling the surface. Use a nontoxic water-based sealer and allow drying time between coats. Some sealers leave a slick coating that keeps adhesive from sticking. If your sealer leaves such a finish, roughen it lightly with sandpaper.

Use a jigsaw or scroll saw to cut curving contours in wood.

CEMENT BOARD

Cement board is sold in 4 x 8-foot (1.2 x 2.4 m) sheets and various thicknesses in building supply stores. Most kinds are made of cement mixed with cellulose or other fibers and are reinforced with synthetic mesh on either side. I look for the kind called tile backerboard, which is used primarily as a base for wall and floor tile installations, because it's waterproof. For most projects I use the ½-inch (1.3 cm) thickness.

You can cut cement board into sections, much as you would a sheet of plywood. For straight cuts, a heavy-duty utility knife is all you need. Just cut the board on one side, cutting through the mesh as well as the cement. Then snap the board along the cut line and cut the mesh on the other side with the utility knife to separate the pieces. For cutting complex shapes the best

tool is a power spiral saw with a ceramic tile-cutting bit. You can also cut cement board with a conventional hand saw or jigsaw, but the material quickly dulls the blade. No matter what tool you use, wear a dust mask to keep from breathing cement particles.

Cutting cement board leaves a rough edge. To level the edge for tiling, brush on a coating of cement slurry, then smooth a layer of fiber cement over the ragged surface (photos above).

Suzan Germond, *Sunshine*, 2000, 24 inches diameter (61 cm), terra cotta mold, stained glass, gold tile, gems. Photo by artist.

EPOXY PUTTY

Epoxy putty is sold in the plumbing section of building supply stores. I use it both as an adhesive for joining sections of concrete board and as a sculptural material over wire armatures. The putty is packaged in a cylindrical plastic tube and consists of two parts: a dark gray center inside a white outer layer. Always wear latex gloves while working with the material. To use it, twist off the amount you want and knead the putty until the two layers are thoroughly combined and a uniform color (photo top middle). The kneading activates the hardener—the putty becomes warm as the chemicals combine. Once the epoxy is mixed, you have a working time of about 10 minutes; you must apply and smooth the putty and remove any excess before it hardens. After 10 minutes the material is difficult to work, and within 20 minutes it turns steel-hard. Some kinds of epoxy putty come in rolls (they look like cinnamon rolls because of the layers) but they're not as easy to work as the tube putty.

To join sections of cement board with epoxy putty, knead the epoxy to activate it, then roll it to form a "snake" the length of the pieces you're joining. Press the snake along the edge of one piece of cement board, then push the other board's edge into the epoxy. Use a clay modeling tool to work the putty into the joint on both sides. Then roll another snake of putty and press it into the joint as needed to reinforce the bond (photo bottom middle). Hold the pieces in place until the putty hardens.

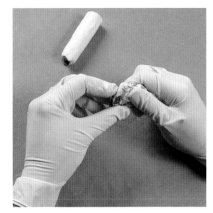

While wearing gloves, knead epoxy putty until the two layers are thoroughly combined.

Use epoxy putty to join sections of cement board.

I use other types of epoxy for certain situations. Marine epoxy—which comes in two parts and must be mixed—is valuable for reinforcing areas on large wire armatures where two parts come together. For small jobs when I need just a dab of epoxy, I use the form that comes in a syringe.

Craigie, *Rebirth,* 2000, 10 feet tall (3 m), slumped glass, stained glass, ceramic tile, mirror on wooden base. Photo by Evan Bracken.

POLYMER SCULPTURING COMPOUND

Several of the projects in this book start with bases created from polymer sculpturing compound, a pliable material that can be molded and shaped like clay, but that's also easier to use and exceptionally durable. Unlike natural clay, which consists of mineral particles suspended in water, polymer compound is made from finely pulverized polyvinyl chloride (PVC) mixed with a plasticizer. It can be fired in an ordinary oven. Not all polymer compounds are the same, however—some kinds are stiff and require conditioning to make them pliant; others become brittle after being fired.

For outdoor mosaic projects, avoid the kinds sold in many colors and small square portions (usually called *polymer clay*). Instead, look for the type that's widely sold in craft stores in 1-pound (454 g) packages and can also be purchased by mail or over the Internet in 8- and 24-pound (3.6 and 10.9 kg) packages. The material is skin-colored and is often described as "ceramic-like." It's workable right out of the box, and when baked is shatter- and chip-resistant and so hard you can sand it, drill it—and mosaic it.

Important Tips for Using Polymer Compound

When using polymer compound, remember these guidelines and precautions:

Polymer compound is synthetic, not to be ingested. Don't snack while working with it, and be careful that a child or pet doesn't eat it. Scrub your hands thoroughly after using the material.

Knead the material thoroughly before shaping it, to ensure the plasticizer is distributed evenly.

Bake the compound on a baking sheet reserved only for this purpose. Don't use the same baking sheet for food. This also goes for any utensils you may use.

Consider buying a toaster oven especially for baking polymer compound. If you use your home oven, afterward wash the inside thoroughly with water and baking soda to remove any residue.

Follow the manufacturer's instructions for firing temperatures and times. Most recommend firing at 250° F or 275° F (121° C or 135° C) for 20 minutes for every $1/4$ inch (6 mm) of thickness. I preheat my oven; others don't. Just make sure that the material bakes for the full time at the right temperature.

Keep a window open and the room ventilated during baking.

Don't let the polymer compound burn by baking it too long or at too high a temperature. If the polymer becomes hotter than 300° F (149° C), the PVC burns and gives off toxic fumes. For this reason always use an oven thermometer to make sure your oven isn't hotter than the temperature set on the dial.

After baking, turn off the oven, open the door, and let the items cool gradually before removing them.

When the pieces have cooled and can be handled, if you can feel any flexibility or give at all, heat the oven again and return the pieces to bake for 15 additional minutes or until they're properly hardened.

Always wear a dust mask when sanding fired polymer compound.

Armature- and Base-Building Techniques

Several of this book's projects incoporate unique bases. The instructions that follow not only help you build them, but also demonstrate techniques you can adapt when creating other works.

BUILDING A SIMPLE PLANT SURROUND BASE

A simple conical armature made of window screen covered with fiber cement produces a versatile base you can mosaic any way you choose. Both the Ceramic Tile Plant Surround on page 69 and the Spiraling Pebbles Plant Surround on page 109 start with this base.

Materials

1 sheet of poster board, at least
    20 x 20 inches (50.8 x 50.8 cm)
2 x 2-foot (61 x 61 cm) piece of
    wire window screen
Plastic sheeting or cling wrap
Cement slurry (page 25)
1 ½ batches of Basic Fiber Cement
    (page 25)

Tools and Supplies

15 inches (38 cm) of string
Pencil
Ruler
Thumbtack
Compass
Scissors
Permanent marker
Stapler
Potter's rib or 3 x 4-inch rectangle
    (7.6 cm x 10.2 cm) cut from
    plastic milk jug

Laying out the Base

1 Copy a surround template from page 140 or page 148, and transfer the outer and inner circles (see page 41) to the poster board, then proceed to step 5. Or follow steps 2 through 4 to draw circles directly on the poster board.

2 To create a makeshift compass for drawing the large outer circle, tie one end of the string to the pencil. Then measure 9 ½ inches (24.1 cm) out from the pencil and stick a thumbtack through the string at that point.

3 With the thumbtack in the middle of the poster board and the string extended move the pencil 360 degrees, draw a circle 19 inches (48.3 cm) in diameter (photo 1).

4 Use the real compass to draw a circle 6 ¾ inches (17.1 cm) in diameter in the middle of the large circle.

5 With both circles on the poster board, use a ruler and pencil to draw a vertical line through the circles' middle. Then draw a horizontal line through the middle, forming crosshairs (photo 2).

6 Cut the large circle out of the poster board.

7 Place the circle on the wire mesh or screen. Trace around it with permanent marker, and then cut around the mark to make a wire circle the same size (photo 3).

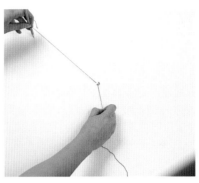

Photo 1

Photo 2

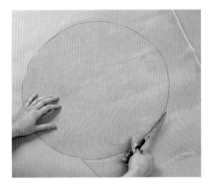

Photo 3

Photo 4

Photo 5

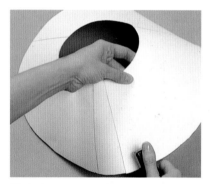

Photo 6

Photo 7

8 Cut along one line from the poster board circle's edge to the small inner circle. Then cut around the small circle and remove it (photo 4).

9 Place the poster board circle over the wire circle and trace around the inner hole with a permanent marker. Then, using a ruler, draw a line from the wire circle's outside edge to the marked inner circle.

10 Repeat step 8 with the wire circle; cut along the line to the inner circle, then cut and remove the small circle.

11 Lay the poster board circle in front of you with the cut to the center vertical, at the six o'clock position. Mark the inner circle ¾ inch (1.9 cm) below its intersection with the left horizontal line (photo 5).

Making the Base

12 Overlap the poster board circle's cut edge until it aligns with the mark, forming a cone. With the top and bottom edges even, staple in place (photo 6).

13 Place the wire mesh over the paper cone and overlap its cut edge to create the same size cone, fitting perfectly atop the poster board. Align the bottom and top edges, and staple the screen cone together. Do not staple it to the poster board cone, which is only a temporary form and not a part of the wire armature (photo 7).

Photo 8

Photo 9

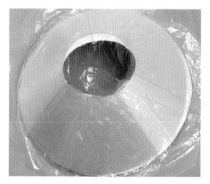

Photo 10

14 Cover the paper cone with plastic sheeting or cling wrap (photo 8). Then place the screen cone atop the plastic (photo 9).

15 Paint a coating of cement slurry on the wire cone (photo 10).

Photo 11

Photo 12

Photo 13

Photo 14

16 Carefully press and smear on and into the screen a ³⁄₈-inch (9.5 mm) layer of fiber cement. Reach inside the cone with one hand to support it as you work (photo 11). Brush on more slurry, if necessary, to keep the area you're about to cement wet. Smooth the cement layer with the potter's rib or plastic rectangle (photo 12). Make sure the top lip and lower edge also are smooth and of even thickness (photos 13 and 14). No screen should be showing through in any spot.

17 Cover the base with plastic and let it cure three to five days (photo 15).

Timmerman Daugherty, Flower on Acid, 2001, 28 x 18 x 18 inches (71.1 x 45.7 x 45.7 cm), stained glass, mirror, marbles, ceramic pieces, found objects. Photo by John Lehr.

Photo 15

FORMING A CONTOURED ARMATURE AND MODELED FACE

To create complex three-dimensional sculptured objects for mosaicking, build a structural skeleton first, use wire mesh to define contours, and then add surface material such as fiber cement. For example, here's how to create the base for the Multi-Faceted Gazing Face project on page 116.

Materials

Multi-Faceted Gazing Face profile pattern (page 150)
5 feet (1.5 m) of 6-gauge (4 mm) armature wire
15 feet (4.6 m) of 20-gauge (.75 mm) aluminum wire
Form-holding woven wire mesh, 2 ½ x 2 ½ feet (75 x 75 cm)
Ingredients for 2 batches of slurry (page 25)
Ingredients for 2 batches of Basic Fiber Cement (page 25)

Tools and Supplies

Needle-nose pliers
Wire cutters
Fiber Cement Supply Kit (page 25)

Shaping the Wire Face

1 Cut a 24-inch (61 cm) length of 6-gauge (4 mm) armature wire. Using needle-nose pliers and following the Gazing Face profile pattern (or a tracing of it), bend the wire to create a facial profile (photo 1). Leave at least 4 inches (10.2 cm) of extra wire at each end, measuring from the top of the face and from the chin.

2 Bend the remaining 36 inches (90 cm) of 6-gauge (4 mm) armature wire into an 11-inch-long (27.9 cm) face-shaped oval measuring 8 inches (20.3 cm) across at its widest point, which is 5 inches (12.7 cm) down from the top of the head. Wrap one end of the wire around the other at the base, or chin, to complete the oval. Trim off excess with wire cutters. Then attach the profile wire to the oval, wrapping and trimming the wire at each end (photo 2).

3 Now wrap lengths of 20-gauge (.75 mm) wire across the face and profile wire, creating a support structure. Start by wrapping one end of a piece of 20-gauge wire around the oval wire near the top of the head, about 2 inches (5 cm) to the left of where the profile wire is attached. Then stretch the 20-gauge wire straight across to the profile wire, wrap it around a couple of times, pull it across to the right side, and wrap it around the oval wire. Now pull it back across to the profile wire 1 inch (2.5 cm) or so lower, wrap it around a couple of times, stretch it across to the other side of the oval wire—and so on (photo 3). Continue working from one side

to the profile wire to the other side and back, starting new lengths of 20-gauge wire as needed, until the entire face is criss-crossed.

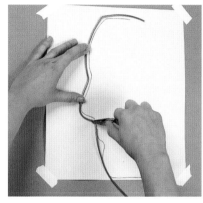

Photo 1

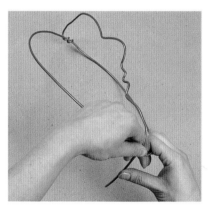

Photo 2

Photo 3

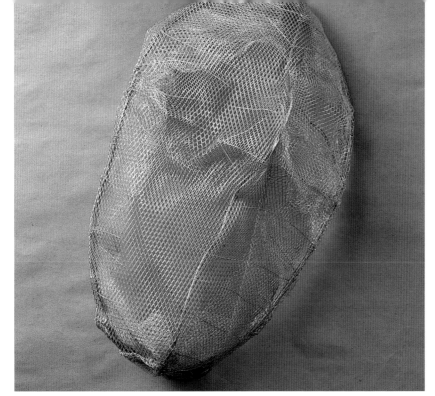

Photo 4

Modeling the Features

4 Fold the wire mesh in half, doubling its thickness. Place the mesh over the wire face. Tuck the top edge over and behind the forehead. Press and form the mesh in place over the nose and the rest of the face. Fold the edges back over the oval wire, up inside the armature (photo 4).

5 Mix one batch of slurry and one batch of fiber cement. Turn the wire armature face-side down and brush slurry onto the entire back side (photo 5). Then press and smooth a layer of fiber cement onto the slurried surface (photo 6).

6 Turn the armature face-side up. Brush it with slurry and begin smoothing on the first facial layer of fiber cement (photo 7).

7 Create basic features by pressing and shaping with your fingertips (photo 8). Look in the mirror at your own face for guidance. Continue adding fiber cement and building up the beginnings of cheeks, lips, eyebrows, nose, and chin (photo 9) until you've used up the first batch of fiber cement. Wrap the face in plastic and let it set overnight.

Photo 5

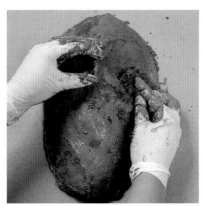

Photo 7

Photo 6

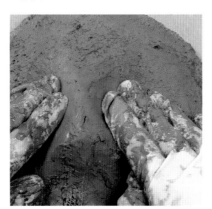

Photo 8

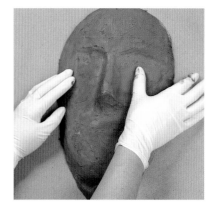

Photo 9

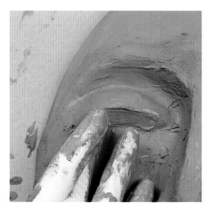

Photo 10

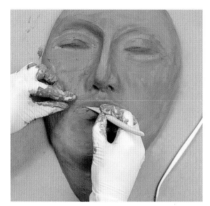

Photo 11

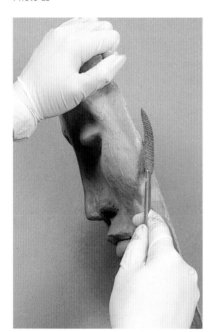

Photo 12

8 Unwrap the face and mix another batch of slurry and fiber cement. Turn the face over, brush slurry on the surface, and fill the backside to the level of the oval wire with more cement. Then turn the face right side up, brush slurry onto the surface, and add another layer of fiber cement, concentrating on building up facial details (photo 10).

9 Continue adding fiber cement to the face, smoothing the surface nicely and creating a total thickness (both layers) of ½ to 1 inch (1.3 to 2.5 cm). Use your fingers and clay modeling tools to sculpt and refine the eyes, nose, and lips (photo 11). Make sure no wires or wire mesh are showing.

10 Wrap the face in plastic and let the fiber cement cure for three to five days. Unwrap and use a rasp to file away the edge created where the cement and work surface were in contact (photo 12).

Virginia Bullman & LaNelle Davis, *The Millworker*, 2000-2001, 7 x 4 x 4 feet (2.1 x 1.2 x 1.2 m), hyper-tufa concrete sculpture over rebar armature, found broken dish mosaic. Photo by Seth Tice-Lewis.

BUILDING A WIRE BRANCH AND FLOWER

You can create all sorts of shapes using flexible (copper, brass, or aluminum) wire. Then cover the wire with epoxy putty to provide a surface for tiling. For example, here's how to make the branch and flower for the Reflecting Bird Bath with View on page 130.

Materials and Tools

6 feet (1.8 m) of 18-gauge (1 mm) flexible wire
6 feet (1.8 m) of 26-gauge (0.41 mm) flexible wire
2 feet (0.6 m) of 11-gauge (2.3 mm) steel cable wire
Wire cutters
Needle-nose pliers
Rubber gloves
Epoxy putty

Shaping the Wires

1 Cut one 9-inch (22.9 cm) and two 7-inch (17.8 cm) lengths of steel cable wire.

2 At one end of each 7-inch (17.8 cm) piece, unwrap the first inch (2.5 cm) or so of cable wire and spread apart the smaller wires into two or three groups, making the end look a bit like a bird's foot (photo 1). Wrap the "foot" of one 7-inch (17.8 cm) cable around the 9-inch (22.9 cm) cable wire about 3 inches (7.6 cm) from one end, and the other 7-inch section about 7 inches from the same end, so the two smaller branches are 4 inches (10.2 cm) apart (photo 2). Bend the small branches so they're roughly parallel to each other, angling off from the main branch.

3 Use the 18-gauge (1 mm) wire to fashion two 2-inch-long (5 cm) leaves, two 1-½-inch (3.8 cm) leaves, and four 1-¼-inch (3.2 cm) leaves. Also make five 1-½-inch (3.8 cm) petals, making them appropriately wider and more rounded. Always keep some extra wire at the end of each petal and leaf, for attaching to the branch (photo 3).

4 Use the 26-gauge (0.41 mm) wire to wrap and criss-cross each leaf and petal, filling in some of the empty space in the centers to create small wire armatures that epoxy can grab (photo 4).

5 By wrapping the extra wire at the end of each leaf, attach one 1 ¼-inch (3.2 cm) and one 1 ½-inch (3.8 cm) leaf an inch (2.5 cm) or so up the first small branch—(the cable wire you affixed 3 inches (7.6 cm) from the main branch's end). Attach another 1-¼-inch (3.2 cm) leaf at the tip of that branch. Then wrap a 1-¼-inch (3.2 cm) leaf near the tip of the other small branch, and a 1-½-inch (3.8 cm) leaf just below that (see photo 9 on the next page).

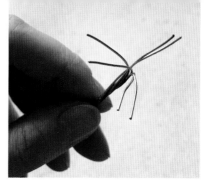

Photo 1

Photo 2

Photo 3

Photo 4

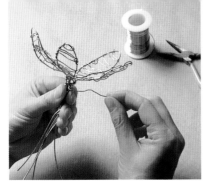

Photo 5

Photo 6

Photo 7

Photo 8

Photo 9

6 Wire the five flower petals together (photo 5), then secure the flower and the two 2-inch (5 cm) leaves at the juncture of the main branch and second, or outermost, small branch. Be sure all the branches, leaves, and petals are wrapped tightly to the main branch. Snip off any wire ends that may be sticking up (photo 6).

Sculpting the Branches, Leaves, and Flowers

7 Now it's time to sculpt the branches, leaves, and flower with epoxy putty. Wear latex gloves while handling the epoxy to protect your hands. Start by pulling off and kneading two ½-inch (1.3 cm) pieces of putty until they're a uniform color. Beginning at the base of the main branch, wrap and press the epoxy around the wire, creating a uniform ⅛-inch-thick (3 mm) layer (photo 7).

8 Continue kneading and applying small batches of epoxy, keeping the surface as smooth as possible. Use a modeling tool to push the putty into hard-to-reach areas (photo 8). Work your way outward, covering everything—branches, leaves, and flower petals (photo 9). Make sure no wires are showing or sticking up through the putty. If there's any play in the branches, or if one part cracks while you're working on another part, just reinforce the area with more epoxy.

Photo 1

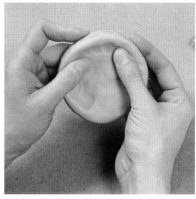

Photo 2

Photo 3

Photo 4

MAKING SIMPLE PINCH POTS

You can always add mosaic to an existing piece of pottery, as I did with the Night and Day Flowerpot on page 122 and also the Sugar-and-Cream Strawberry Planter on page 86. But why limit yourself to just pottery you can buy in a store? Here's how to create freeform pinch pots—which, as you can see from the Sparkling Freeform Pinch-Pot Vases project on page 113, you can make in almost any size or shape. The instructions here are for a medium-size pot; just increase or decrease the amount of compound appropriately to make larger or smaller pots.

Materials and Tools

3/4 pound (252 g) of polymer
   sculpturing compound
Rubber gloves
Baking sheet
1 sheet of 180- or 220-grit
   sandpaper
Dust mask

Instructions

1 Start by rolling one 1/4-pound (114 g) slab of compound into a ball between the palms of your hands (photo 1).

2 Next, flatten the ball into a disc. Press your thumbs into the middle and push outward, creating the beginning of an outer wall all the way around (photo 2).

3 Thin out and bring up the sides by pinching them between your fingers, working around the pot to keep the shape even (photo 3). Don't let the walls become any thinner than 1/4 inch (6 mm).

4 To add material for more height, roll a lump of compound back and forth on a flat surface, forming a long snake or coil (photo 4). Then, starting with one end of the coil and working around the pot, pinch the coil

Photo 5

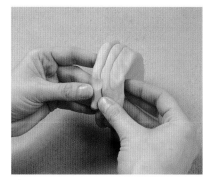

Photo 6

Photo 7

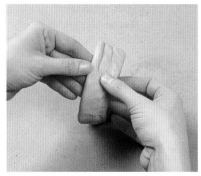

Photo 8

onto the wall (photo 5). Press and smooth the coil firmly, making it a part of the pot (photos 6 and 7). When you come to the end of the coil, roll out another, if needed, and pinch that on—and so forth. Build up the pot pinch by pinch, coil by coil, row by row (photo 8). To widen the pot's diameter, add a coil slightly larger than the clay wall's circumference; to bring the shape back in, add a smaller coil closer to the pot's interior.

5 Once you've achieved the desired size and shape, form the pot's mouth—make it oval, round, rectangular, triangular, whatever. Shaping the mouth simply adds one more level of character. Be sure the pot's lip is smooth and flat, to make tiling easier. To finish the bottom of the pot so it will stand upright, carefully press the base onto a level surface, flattening the underside.

6 Place the pot upright on a baking sheet and, following the instructions and safety precautions on page 28, bake in a preheated oven. Note that if you make more than one vase, bake them one at a time, not together— baking them as a group will take even longer than baking them consecutively.

7 When the pot has finished baking and cooling, sand the surface (remember to wear your dust mask) to remove any major lumps and bumps. You don't have to get carried away here; just smooth the surface enough to ensure that tesserae will lie flat.

Sherri Warner Hunter, *Mr. Inman Tribute,* **1999,** 95 x 26 x 22 inches (241 x 66 x 56 cm), concrete forms, ceramic, glass, in conjunction with the Ensworth School (Nashville, Tennessee). Photo by Gary Layda.

FORMING A POLYMER POD PLANTER

The beauty of polymer sculpturing compound is its versatility. You can form almost any shape imaginable—and add other elements too. Here's the simple method for crafting long-stemmed bases for the Nodding Pod Planters project on page 81.

Materials and Tools

Polymer sculpturing compound
Baking sheet
Epoxy putty
$\frac{1}{8}$-inch diameter (3 mm) steel rod
Wire cutters
Latex gloves

Photo 1

Photo 2

Photo 3

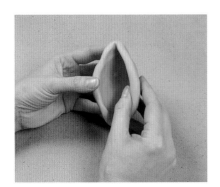

Photo 4

Instructions

1 Roll one ¼-pound (114 g) slab of sculpturing compound into a ball between the palms of your hands (photo 1).

2 Use your thumbs to make an indentation in the ball (photo 2).

3 Pressing and shaping with your thumbs and fingers, form an elongated bowl—this will become a "pod" (photos 3 and 4).

4 Put the pod on a baking sheet and, following the instructions and precautions on page 26, bake in a preheated oven according to the manufacturer's recommendations. When the pod has finished baking, open the oven door and let it cool; then remove it from the oven.

5 Pinch off two ½-inch (1.3 cm) pieces of epoxy putty and knead them until they're an even color (photo 5). Roll the putty into a ball and press it firmly onto the base of the pod (photo 6); then smooth it, forming a thick cone (photo 7).

6 Push one end of a length of steel rod (the pod's support) into the putty and bring the putty down around the top ¾ inch (1.9 cm) of rod, tapering it to a funnel-like point (photo 8). Hold the pod and rod in position for several minutes until the putty hardens. Make sure there's no wobble or give; if there is, knead and add more putty.

Photo 5

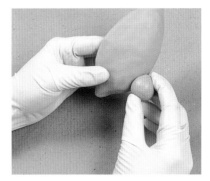

Photo 6

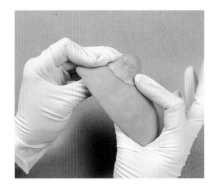

Photo 7

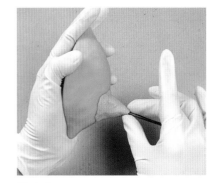

Photo 8

FIGURE 1

DO:

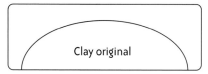

Slope sides outward

DON'T:

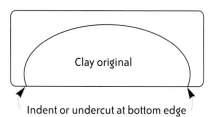

Indent or undercut at bottom edge

Photo 1

Photo 2

CREATING A MOLD FOR MAKING MULTIPLES

For some projects, you'll want to make more than just one of a small base or sculpture. This technique allows you to use a single object to create a plaster mold for making multiples of the original.

Materials and Tools

Natural clay (such as potter's clay)
Clay modeling tools
Plastic food storage container
Plaster of Paris
Spray cooking oil
Fiber cement

Instructions

1 Using clay and clay modeling tools, sculpt the desired base object (such as a beetle for the Bold Beautiful Beetle project on page 106). Keep the design simple, with gradual contours and a smooth surface, to make tiling easier.

2 Check the sides and under-side of the sculpture. The sides should slope outward to the bottom. There must be no undercuts or indentations along the bottom edge or cast objects will become locked in the resulting mold (see figure 1).

3 Place the sculpture bottom-side-down in the container. The container should be at least 1 inch (2.5 cm) larger on all four sides than the sculpture, and about 2 inches (5 cm) deeper than the object's height. Press gently along the sculpture's bottom edge to seal off any gaps that might allow plaster to creep beneath the sculpture.

4 Mix the plaster of Paris according to the manufacturer's directions and pour it into the plastic container, filling it to a depth of 1 inch (2.5 cm) above the sculpture (photo 1). Tap and shake the container lightly to get rid of trapped air bubbles. Let the plaster set up overnight.

5 Cut away and discard the plastic container. Then remove the sculpture from the mold. If it's stuck, pry it out gently with a pencil or other tool, taking care not to scar the plaster. Wipe out any remaining clay sticking to the walls of the mold.

6 To cast a replica using the mold, spray the inside surface thoroughly with cooking oil. The oil will act as a release agent, allowing you to remove the cast beetle once it has hardened. Mix enough fiber cement to fill the mold and press the material into it, pushing out any trapped air. Wrap the cement-filled mold in plastic and leave it overnight. Then remove the cast object from the mold (photo 2). Wrap it in plastic and let the cement cure for three to five days.

CHAPTER THREE

The Mosaic Process

Pearse Kelly, *Technicolor Dreampot,* **2001,**
36 x 18 inches (91.4 m x 45.7 cm), terra cotta
urn, colored ceramic and porcelain tile, finished with colored, sanded grout and sealant.
Photo by artist.

Learning to mosaic, like learning to do almost anything else,
is an ongoing affair. It's a matter
of practice to perfect skills and a
matter of time and experience to
develop your own style, your own
senses of color and design, your
own ways of approaching a project.
Don't be afraid to just plunge in.
One of the beauties of mosaic is
that it's a most forgiving medium.

Transferring Patterns

Sometimes I'll draw a design
directly onto an object I'm about
to mosaic (photo right), and then
place tesserae between the lines.
Other times I'll just start with a
general design in my mind and let
the idea materialize and evolve as I
cut, shape, and place the pieces.

You'll develop your own
favorite working style over time.
At some point, though—and
maybe especially when you're just
beginning—you'll want to transfer
an existing design onto an object
to use as a template, or guideline,
for your mosaic. I've provided
template patterns in this book
(starting on page 137) for many
of the projects.

To transfer a pattern, you'll
need the materials listed for the
Pattern Transfer Kit on the next
page. Note that black graphite

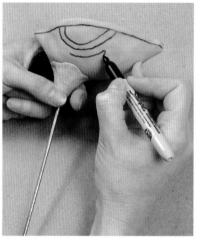

For some projects you can draw a pattern
directly onto the object. You may want to
sketch a design in pencil first, and then go
over the lines with marker once you're
happy with the design.

paper is *not* the same as carbon
paper for typing, but a special,
wax-free paper sold in crafts and
art supply stores specifically for
transferring designs.

For many of the project patterns, you'll also need to enlarge
the design by the percentage
indicated on the page in order to
produce a full-size template.
Most photocopiers have this
capability. If the design is particularly large—larger than the
copying machine's paper—you
may need to copy the pattern in
sections, and then tape the
enlarged copies together. In some
cases you may also need to
enlarge the design a second time,
as indicated on the template.

Pattern Transfer Kit

Tracing paper
Pencil (2B)
Black graphite paper
  (if indicated in project)
Masking or cellophane tape
Black permanent marker

Photo 1

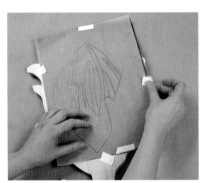

Photo 2

Photo 3

TRANSFERRING PATTERNS ONTO FLAT OBJECTS

1 Trace the pattern template using tracing paper slightly larger than the pattern itself. Be sure to make good, solid lines as you trace.

2 Tape the tracing paper pencil-side up against the back (non-graphite side) of a matching-size or larger piece of graphite paper (photo 1).

3 Put the joined papers graphite-side down on the surface of the object you want to transfer the pattern to. With the template properly aligned, tape the papers in place to keep them from slipping (photo 2).

4 Now carefully go over all of the lines on the tracing paper with a pencil. Apply enough pressure to transfer the image through the graphite, but not so much that you rip or tear the papers. Begin in one clearly defined spot and move methodically through the pattern, paying attention to where you are and making sure to cover every line (photo 3). Try not to stop midway though the process, because you may not be able to tell where you were when you stopped. If you remove the graphite paper and discover that part of the design wasn't transferred, you'll have to try to put the graphite paper back on the object in the same place—a difficult task because you can't see through the graphite paper to align the pattern.

Photo 4

Photo 5

5 Once you've finished transferring the design, carefully remove the papers (photo 4) and go over the graphite lines with a permanent marker so that the pattern can't be smudged or erased (photo 5).

Linda Wallen, *1208 Mosaic*, **1998-2000,** tile, broken china, found objects, handmade tile pieces. Photo by artist.

TRANSFERRING PATTERNS ONTO THREE-DIMENSIONAL OBJECTS

Transferring a pattern onto a flat surface is relatively easy, but on more complicated surfaces you can't always position and trace over an entire pattern all at once. Instead, you'll have to work in sections.

For instance, to transfer a pattern to the curved surface of a flowerpot, first tape the top of the joined tracing/graphite papers to a portion of the top edge of the flowerpot, leaving the sides and bottom of the paper loose but making sure that the pattern would be aligned evenly if it was wrapped all the way around. Then smooth down the paper in the center of the section facing you, where the flowerpot contacts the graphite paper directly, and trace the lines in that section. Next, turn the flowerpot slightly, smooth down and trace over the next section (which is now facing you), and so on. Reposition the tape along the top edge as needed to keep the section you're working on in place. Continue turning, smoothing, and tracing until the entire design has been transferred. Then remove the paper and go over the lines with permanent marker.

Cutting Techniques

Spend some time experimenting with various cutting techniques and tools. Never mind if you ruin some tiles or glass along the way. That's standard operating procedure—especially when you're just starting out. With practice, you will get good at cutting. Tools that may seem awkward and unfamiliar at first will become useful extensions of your hands. Of course, always remember to wear safety goggles when cutting.

CUTTING SHAPES

For some projects you'll want to cut tesserae into distinct shapes such as circles, triangles, or crescents. Using glass mosaic cutters, you can cut these shapes from vitreous glass tiles or from stained glass or mirror tiles you've made yourself (see page 19).

To make rectangles, cut a square straight in half (photo 1); to make tiny squares, halve the rectangles (photo 2). Make triangles by cutting a tile in half diagonally; then cut the two halves diagonally in the opposite direction to make small equilateral triangles (photo 3).

Photo 1

Photo 2

Photo 3

Photo 4

Photo 5

Photo 6

Photo 7

To create curved shapes, use glass mosaic cutters to nip a series of slight angles at the corners and along the edges of tiles. To make crescent moon shapes, nibble away the outside corners and middle of triangles (photo 4). To create a circle, nip a series of angles around a square tile, removing small bits at a time to form a smooth, even curve (photos 5 and 6).

You can also use these techniques with ceramic tile nippers to shape vitreous glass tiles. The cut edges will be somewhat more ragged, creating tesserae with a looser look. Of course, tile nippers are *the* tool to use when shaping pieces of ceramic tile. By carefully lining up the jaws in the direction of the cuts you want to make, you can create basic shapes such as triangles (photo 7). Breaking 4 x 4-inch (10.2 x 10.2 cm) tiles into shards with a hammer, and then nipping them into smaller, more precise shapes to fill available space is a simple and quick way to work.

Jan Hinson, *Queen of Cups Throne,* **1997,** 48 x 40 inches (122 x 102 cm), lightweight ferro-cement forms, reset broken tile.
Photo by artist.

Cutting a Simple Leaf Shape

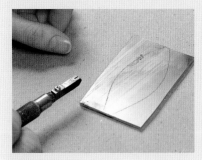 

1 Start with a piece of glass as long as and slightly wider than the leaf you want to create. Using a glasscutter, score an arc from the middle of one narrow end to the middle of the other. Then score a matching arc on the other side.

3 Score and snap the leaf shape in half lengthwise.

4 Using glass mosaic cutters, nip each side evenly into diagonal sections.

5 With the sections spaced slightly apart, the grout lines between will simulate leaf veins.

2 Use running pliers to break the glass at the scores, creating the basic leaf shape.

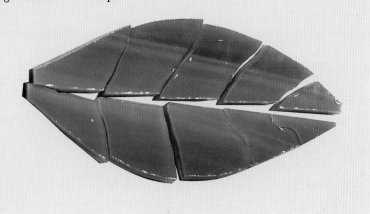

CUTTING IRREGULAR TESSERAE

Notice that in the section on cutting shapes I never mentioned (or showed in the photos) "perfect" squares, triangles, or whatever. That's because I don't like perfect. I think the eye is far more attracted to slight imperfections, to irregular shapes. Even when I make my own square or rectangular tiles as described on page 19, I sometimes vary the widths of the strips I score and break off, and then snip them with glass mosaic cutters into slightly angled pieces of varying size, each unique (photo below). Irregular tesserae or shards with interesting curves or angles add visual impact.

To create slightly irregular stained glass tiles, use glass mosaic cutters to nip strips into not-quite-perfect squares or rectangles.

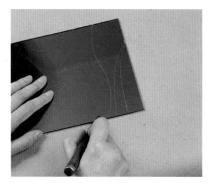
Photo 1

Photo 2

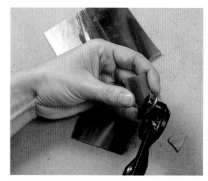
Photo 3

A glasscutter is great for creating shards with long, sweeping curves. Just score the glass or mirror freehand (photo 1), then break off the pieces with running pliers (photo 2).

More than any other method, I favor using glass mosaic cutters to cut and shape irregular, fractured-looking shards of stained glass (photo 3). I often use this method when filling in

or tiling areas around design details, as shown in the series of four photos, below left. Cutting and adding irregular tesserae to a surface is like doing a jigsaw puzzle, only you get to shape the pieces as you go, to make them fit together however you wish. The glass mosaic cutters can create slight curves in the shards as well as angled cuts, which allows you to shape them to conform to the space you want to fill while maintaining their overall fractured appearance.

You can also use this technique with vitreous glass and ceramic tiles. The irregular shards you get from vitreous tiles will have a more angular look and feel, simply because you start with perfect squares. Ceramic tile, dinnerware, and china cut into shards with nippers have a heavier, broken-plate appearance.

When working with irregular shards, use glass mosaic cutters to cut pieces to the approximate sizes you need.

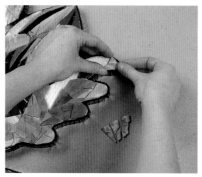
Shape the shards as necessary as you place them, to fit the base's contours.

Adding the pieces is a bit like doing a jigsaw puzzle.

You cut and shape the pieces as you go—so they always fit together.

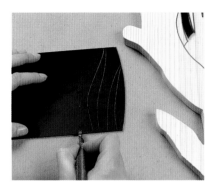

Photo 1

Tiling Techniques

The process of placing and fitting tesserae, of creating a coherent design from disjointed pieces, is the essence of mosaic. Patience, practice, trial and error, give-and-take all play a role. With experience you'll develop an ability to "see" which piece will fit next, which shape will work best.

Before you begin tiling, gather and organize your materials. Cut large sheets of glass or mirror into smaller pieces if that's all you'll need.

Now consider the design. In general I tile design details—such as swirls, spirals, or other important elements—first, then fill in the background areas around them. Once you've decided where to start, begin placing tesserae, shaping them as necessary to fill the area. If you're following a pattern, cut pieces to the approximate sizes and shapes you need (photo 1), and then trim them to fit.

APPLYING ADHESIVE

To apply adhesive, many mosaicists use a flat knife or craft stick to spread glue or mortar onto the back of each piece before placing it, a technique called *buttering*—like spreading butter on a cracker. When using silicone glue, however, I butter only very large pieces. Buttering smaller tesserae with glue is messy and time-consuming. Instead, spread the adhesive directly onto the area you're tiling. For gluing small areas, use the tube's applicator tip to apply and spread the adhesive (photo 2), then press the piece into place (photo 3). Or use a craft stick to spread the glue before positioning the tile (photos 4 and 5).

Keep the adhesive's thickness consistent—about $1/16$ inch (1.6 mm) when working with stained glass or mirror, about $1/8$ inch (3 mm) for other materials. It's difficult to spread the glue evenly so inevitably the glue in some areas will fill the spaces between tesserae; use a dental tool or craft stick to remove it while it's wet. Be careful, too, not to spread glue over an area larger than you can tile before the adhesive dries. If that happens, the tiles won't stick. Placing another layer of glue on top will create an uneven surface. Your only option is to scrape off the dried adhesive and start over. Silicone glue dries in about five to 10 minutes.

When working with thin-set mortar and ceramic tile, butter each piece before placing it. Be sure to cover the entire bottom surface with adhesive, then press it into place. Use a craft stick to remove any excess mortar that oozes out.

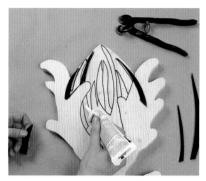

Photo 2

Photo 3

Photo 4

Photo 5

Work upward when tiling vertical surfaces.

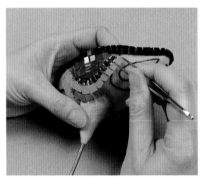
Use proportionately small tesserae when tiling small objects.

Regardless of the adhesive, when tiling vertical surfaces, work from the bottom up. Apply the adhesive, then tile upward, so that the first and lowest pieces you position will help keep the higher pieces from slipping down before their adhesive sets (photo upper left).

PLACING AND SPACING

As you cut and place tesserae, remember these principles:

Keep the spaces between tiles—the gaps that will be filled with grout—consistent as you place them. When using stained glass or vitreous glass tiles, leave between $1/16$ (1.6 mm) and $1/8$ inch (3 mm). When using ceramic tile leave between $1/8$ (3 mm) and $3/16$ inch (5 mm). Narrow grout lines give a piece a tight, controlled look; wider grout lines produce a looser feel.

For small objects, use proportionately small tesserae, positioning and spacing them carefully with tweezers (photo lower left).

When tiling a curved or rounded area, cut or nip the pieces small enough to rest flat on the surface. The greater the curve, the smaller the piece must be cut. If you can rock a piece back and forth, it's too big. Remove it and cut it smaller until, when you reposition it, no movement can be detected.

When tiling adjacent to an edge, place the tesserae flush to the edge, not short of it or extending slightly beyond it. This will create a stronger edge, allowing you to handle the mosaic object more easily, and will also help produce a more even and attractive edge grout line.

Mosaic "Movement"

When cutting and positioning glass or tile to fit a space, fill in a design detail, or conform to an object's shape, pay attention to the "movement" or directional flow you're trying to create or follow. Shape and place the tesserae so that the pieces and the gaps, or negative space, between them "move" in a direction that follows the form or space you're tiling, as shown in the schematic drawings here.

Creating or Following the Movement of the Object You're Tiling

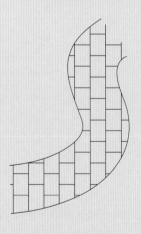
Not following movement

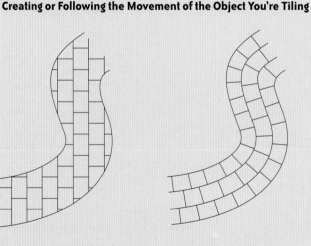
Following movement

Photo 1

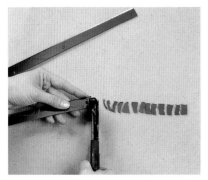
Photo 2

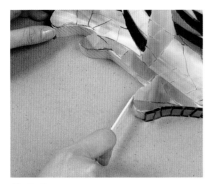
Photo 3

Photo 4

TILING EDGES

Although some mosaic artists recommend otherwise, I always tile the edges of objects. If you tile and grout the edge properly and handle the object carefully (see page 55), you won't have problems with the edge tiles popping off—the main reason why some prefer not to mosaic edges.

To tile an edge, measure the thickness of the base and cut several strips of material to precisely that width. If you make them any larger there won't be enough space for grout in the gap where the edge and surface tiles meet. Use a glass-cutter and running pliers if you're cutting glass or mirror (photo 1). Use a tile cutter if you're working with ceramic tile.

Next, snip the strips into smaller pieces, placing them on your work surface in the order that you cut them. Again, use whichever tool is appropriate to the material: glass mosaic cutters for glass or mirror, tile nippers for ceramic tile. You can cut the pieces into regular or, as shown here, irregular shapes (photo 2). If the edge you're tiling is curved, cut some pieces narrower than others, for tiling along the curves.

Spread adhesive onto a section of edge (photo 3) and press the cut pieces into place, spacing them consistently and taking care to position them flush to both sides of the edge. Make sure that the pieces along curves are narrow enough to lay flat (photo 4); if not, cut them smaller. Use tweezers when tiling tight areas (photo 5).

Continue tiling—cutting and snipping additional strips of material if needed—until the entire edge is finished (photo 6).

Laura Robbins, *Mysterious Peace,* 2001, 16 x 13 ½ x 1 ½ inches (40.6 x 34.2 x 3.8 cm), handmade ceramic tiles, broken glass, lapiz stone mounted on board. Photo by artist.

Photo 5

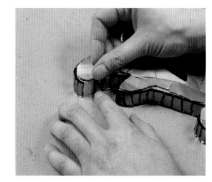
Photo 6

Tiling the lip and inside edge of a vase takes time and patience, but produces a more finished, sophisticated look.

CLEANING ADHESIVE

Before grouting the mosaic, carefully clean away all excess adhesive. Use a craft knife or razor blade to scrape residue from the surface (photo 1). Adhesive in the cracks between tiles will prevent you from filling the gaps properly with grout. Use a craft knife or dental pick (photo 2) to remove the material. This is an important step, so take your time and be careful not to miss any areas.

Use similar techniques to tile the lip and inside edge of flowerpots, vases, and other containers. Often I will carry a design detail and its color from the side of an object over onto the lip and inside edge (photo above).

Note that it's important, when tiling the edges of a flat project, to keep the object flat on the work surface so that the freshly glued tiles will be supported from underneath, preventing them from sliding downward.

Also, once you start tiling edges be careful not to move the piece too soon, or you'll knock off some of the tiles. If you need to turn the object midway through tiling, let the adhesive dry first. Then grasp the piece on the portions of edge that aren't yet tiled, lift it straight up, turn it, and let it down flat. Do not slide the piece.

Photo 1

Photo 2

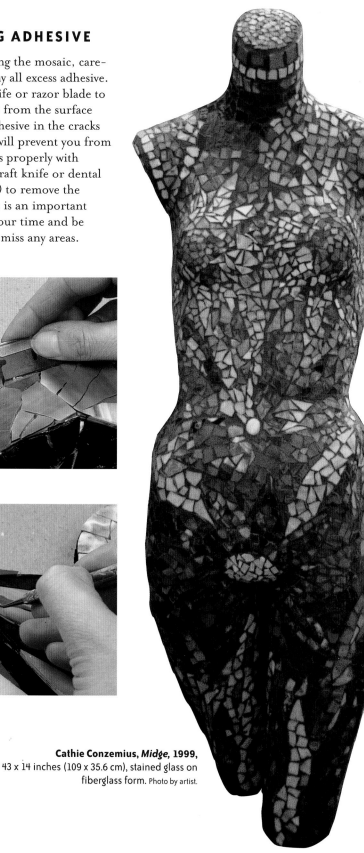

Cathie Conzemius, *Midge,* **1999,** 43 x 14 inches (109 x 35.6 cm), stained glass on fiberglass form. Photo by artist.

Grouting

Grout must be mixed just before you actually apply it to the mosaic, so you need to prepare for both mixing and grouting in advance. Keep in mind, too, that once you start grouting you can't stop midway; you have to complete the process. Make sure you've allowed enough time.

Cover your work surface with plastic or kraft paper. Assemble the materials you'll need—grout, acrylic grout fortifier, and pigment (if you intend to custom-color your grout)—along with the necessary tools and supplies (see page 22).

COLORING AND MIXING

Pour the grout into the mixing container. Add liquid pigment or other colorant next if you're custom-coloring the grout, and, while wearing latex gloves, mix it into the dry material (photo 1). Then pour in and thoroughly mix the acrylic grout fortifier, adding just a little at a time (photo 2). Use only enough liquid so that, when mixed, the grout has the consistency of thick oatmeal (photo 3). When you scoop up a handful and turn your hand over, the grout should slowly glop off. If you mix grout too dry it becomes difficult to work with and may crack off later. If you mix grout too wet it's messy and has no body, making it next to impossible to work with on such areas as edges.

I've included recommended pigment amounts in the projects that call for custom-colored grout. Remember, though, to use your own judgment. You don't have to use the exact amount

Photo 1

Photo 2

Photo 3

specified. It's a good idea, too, to test-grout a spot on the least visible area of the mosaic. If you don't like the way the color looks against the tesserae, wipe the area off with a wet sponge and adjust the color until you do like it. Coloring and mixing grout is like cooking; eventually you develop a "feel" for how much of this and how much of that to add. Keep in mind, too, that you don't *have* to custom-color your grout; just use an acceptable precolored grout if you'd rather.

Photo 4

Photo 5

Photo 6

APPLYING GROUT

Wearing latex gloves, work the mixed grout—a small handful at a time—into the tiled surface (photo 4). Press the grout firmly into the spaces and crevices, rubbing and smoothing it in from all directions (photo 5) until the entire surface is covered and all the gaps are filled (photo 6).

Photo 7

Photo 8

Photo 9

Photo 10

Next, work grout into the edge tiles (photo 7). Then, using your fingers and thumbs, press grout into and along the gap where the surface and edge tiles meet (photo 8). Always take time, too, to work grout along the edge's underside, between the base and the tile ends. Put the project on a block of wood or old book to raise it just enough to get your fingers underneath to smooth grout along this area, strengthening the tiled edge.

Now dip a sponge into the container of water, wring out the water as hard as you can, and wipe excess grout off the tiled surface (photo 9). Be careful not to wipe away too much grout; the material should be level, or nearly so, with the tiles. Rinse and wring out the sponge often as you work; the sponge should be clean and just barely damp. When you've finished the surface, use the sponge to wipe excess grout from the edge tiles and carefully smooth the grout filling the joint between the surface and edge (photo 10). If you wipe away too much grout from this gap, add more and smooth it again.

Photo 11

Photo 12

POLISHING AND CLEANING

Wait several minutes for the surface to haze over as the grout residue dries (photo 11). The bigger the project and the wetter the grout, the longer this will take. Then use a soft cloth to wipe away and polish off the grout haze (photo 12). This is my favorite part of the entire process, not only because it means the project is nearly finished, but also because it's like digging for buried treasure. Wiping away the grout reveals the beauty of the finished piece (photo 13).

As a final step, use a hobby knife, dental pick, razor blade, or clay cleanup tool to scrape away any stubborn spots where dried

Photo 13

Photo 14

grout residue persists on the surface (photo 14). Be careful not to dig out grout between tiles. You want to merely clean the surface of the tile. On the other hand, be careful not to miss any spots. An otherwise fine piece of mosaic looks terrible if it's not cleaned thoroughly.

One other tip: If you're grouting a large piece you may want to work in sections, applying grout to and wiping and polishing each section before moving on to the next. If you try to grout the entire piece at once the grout you apply at the start may harden before you can wipe off the excess with a damp sponge, making it next to impossible to polish and clean the surface.

TWO-TONE GROUTING

For some projects you may want to use a second grout color in an area where the tesserae are a color that's incompatible with the first grout color, or where a second color would simply look good. To do this, you'll need to use masking tape to cover up the edges and other areas where you don't want the first grout color. Be sure to press the tape down firmly, to keep grout from creeping beneath. Use regular masking tape, not the easy-release kind sold to painters; it doesn't have enough adhesive to hold up to the grouting process.

Apply the first grout color and clean and polish the tiles. Wrap the object in plastic and let the grout set overnight. Then carefully remove the masking tape. Now mask off the already-grouted sections and other areas where you don't want the second grout color. You can use plastic sheeting taped in place to cover large areas. Then press tape alongside the outside edges of tiles where you'll be grouting with the second color. Apply the second grout and clean and polish the tiles. Remove the masking tape after the grout has set.

CURING GROUT

Once you've finished grouting, cleaning, and polishing the project it's important to allow the grout to cure properly. Like any cement product grout must be given time to complete the hydration process, which hardens the material.

Wrap the grouted mosaic in plastic sheeting or kraft paper and let the grout set for at least three days. If the grout dries too quickly it may crack, so keep the object out of direct sunlight. Unwrap and check the project after a day; if the grout seems to be drying too quickly spray it lightly with water using a plant mister, then rewrap it. Under hot, dry conditions, you may have to mist it more than once a day.

Sherri Warner Hunter, *Small World Fountain*, 1998, 60 x 24 inches (1.5 m x 61 cm), concrete form, ceramic, glass, stone, shell. Photo by artist.

Photo 1

Photo 2

Photo 3

Photo 4

Indirect Mosaic

Adhering tesserae directly to an object is called, quite sensibly, *direct mosaic*; most of the projects in the book use this approach. Creating a mosaic on a portable surface material, such as fabric mesh, that is then moved and installed elsewhere in a permanent location is known as *indirect mosaic*.

This technique gives you the freedom to put mosaics in all kinds of places outdoors, but allows you to make them indoors, out of the weather and at your own pace. The example here shows the first steps in making the Starburst Garden Appliqué project on page 111, but of course the method can be used for other designs and projects, too.

INDIRECT MOSAIC ON MESH

Materials and Supplies

Plain white paper slightly larger
than the pattern
Masking tape
Ruler
Pencil
Pattern
Pattern Transfer Kit (page 42)
Cling wrap
Fine-weave cotton
latch-hook mesh*
Basic Mosaic Supply Kit
(page 22)
Scissors
Silicone glue
Wide, flat board
Rubber hammer
Plastic sheeting or cut-open
garbage bags
Clay cleanup tool

*Available in fabric stores

1 Tape the paper to your work surface. With a ruler, draw two perpendicular lines (one from top to bottom and the other side to side) intersecting in the paper's center, creating crosshairs. Then add two lines on the diagonals, creating a grid divided into pie-piece shapes.

2 Transfer the pattern to the paper (see page 41), aligning it with the crosshairs. Tape plastic sheeting or cling wrap over the paper (photo 1).

3 Cut the mesh to the same size as or slightly larger than the pattern. Then center the mesh over the plastic-topped design and tape it in place, with the mesh's grid aligned to the vertical and horizontal crosshairs.

4 Place tiles in the center first and work outward. Use glass mosaic cutters to nip pieces to shape as needed (photo 2).

5 Glue the glass pieces and other mosaic materials in place one at a time (photos 3 and 4) until you've filled in the pattern. Let the glue on the completed mosaic dry overnight.

6 Carefully lift the tiled mesh off the cling wrap and, using scissors, trim away the extra mesh around the edges. Cut as close to the tiles as possible.

7 With a helper if necessary, hold the mesh-backed mosaic in place on the wall or other surface where you'll be installing it and trace around the mesh with a pencil. Then spread an even layer of adhesive within the tracing. (If the surface is painted or especially smooth, rough it up with sandpaper first.)

8 Press the mesh-backed mosaic into position in the glue, getting it properly aligned right away, before the adhesive dries too much. (It's helpful to have another person standing behind you to tell you whether the mosaic is positioned correctly.)

9 Place a flat board over the mosaic and with a hammer tap lightly all over the surface to ensure that the entire piece is securely embedded and level. Using dental picks or a razor blade, clean away any adhesive that has come up through the mesh onto the tiles. Let the glue dry for 24 hours. (Cover the mosaic with plastic if rain threatens.)

10 Using masking tape, mask off the edges around the mosaic, leaving an even ¼ inch (6 mm) between the mosaic and tape, for grout. Use the tape's edge to create straight lines, and scissors to snip the tape to fit angles. Press the tape down firmly, especially if you're taping on a rough or uneven surface. Cover the area below the mosaic with plastic so falling excess grout won't stain the surface (photo 5).

11 Grout the mosaic (photo 6).

Photo 5

Photo 6

12 When the grout is semi-set, use a clay cleanup tool to carve a beveled edge along the outside grout lines, slanting the grout from the level of the top of the glass down to the inside edge of tape. Don't wait too long to do this; if the grout has dried completely it will be difficult to carve. Usually, by the time you've finished actually grouting a piece the section you first grouted is ready to bevel.

13 Carefully remove the tape and plastic and clean and polish the mosaic. If any grout crept under the masking tape, clean away as much as possible and touch up the messy edges with a fine paintbrush and paint that matches the surface.

Handling and Caring for Finished Mosaic Objects

Mosaic objects should be handled carefully, not only during construction but also afterward. Here are some tips to keep in mind.

Unless you're wearing gloves, don't run your hands carelessly across the surface of a mosaic. Just one protruding tile edge is enough to cut you.

Never lean a mosaic on edge. This places the weight of the entire piece on that spot and risks popping off some tiles.

Pick mosaic objects straight up, and set them down the same way. If you must tilt a piece—for example, to put soil in the cups of the Cascading Planter on page 119—rest that edge on a cushion or folded towel.

To prolong the life of outdoor mosaic objects, bring them indoors if you can when cold weather approaches, and keep them there until the following spring. Even frostproof mosaics will live longer if you give them shelter in freezing weather.

CHAPTER FOUR

The Projects

Now for the fun part. The 22 projects that follow vary in complexity, style, and materials. If you're a beginner, just choose one of the simpler mosaics and take the plunge. Remember to be patient with yourself; it takes time and experience to acquire the skills you'll need for some of the more difficult projects. Most important, have a good time discovering the pleasures of mosaic—and the creative spirit within you.

Looking Glass Garden Stake

On one side, a lovely mosaic flower; on the other side—surprise!—your garden's

own plants, reflected in sparkling mirror. Cut curving shards of colored mirror

and stained glass freehand to create the blossom's delicate petals.

Materials

12 x 24-inch (30.5 x 61 cm) piece
of ¾-inch (1.9 cm) rot-resistant
wood (see page 26)
Wood sealer

Stained glass:
1 6 x 8-inch (15.2 x 20.3 cm)
piece of red-orange mix
1 6 x 8-inch (15.2 x 20.3 cm)
piece of rose
2 12 x 12-inch (30.5 x 30.5 cm)
sheets of blue-green-yellow mix

1 12 x 12-inch (30.5 x 30.5 cm)
sheet of silver mirror
1 12 x 12-inch (30.5 x 30.5 cm)
sheet of green mirror
1 12 x 12-inch (30.5 x 30.5 cm)
sheet of blue mirror
Silicone glue
3 pounds (1.4 kg) of blue
sanded grout
1 ½ ounces (45 mL) of yellow
liquid pure pigment
Acrylic grout fortifier

Tools and Supplies

Pattern for Looking Glass Garden
Stake (page 137)
Pattern Transfer Kit (page 42)
Jigsaw or scroll saw
Sandpaper
Paintbrush
Ring saw
Glass mosaic cutters
Tile-Making Kit (page 19)
Towel or cushion
Basic Mosaic Supply Kit
(page 22)

Instructions

Note: Many of the steps involved in making this project are shown in photos on pages 46 through 53 of Chapter 3.

1 Transfer the stake's outline and mirror side pattern to the wooden board (see page 42). Be sure to go over the graphite lines with permanent marker.

2 Using a jigsaw or scroll saw, carefully cut out the stake. Sand any rough edges smooth.

3 Now transfer the blossom design to the other side of the stake. Again, go over the graphite lines with a permanent marker.

4 Apply two coats of outdoor wood sealer to the entire stake, including the edges, allowing drying time between coats. (You may have to do just one side and the edges first, then the other side.) Let the stake dry completely overnight.

TILING THE BLOSSOM SIDE

5 You'll tile the blossom side first. Lay the stake on your work surface with the blossom design facing up. Following the pattern on the stake while using the glasscutter to score the pieces and running pliers to snap them free, cut and glue long slivers of green mirror for the flower bud. You can sketch these sliver shapes onto the mirror with a marker and then cut them, but it's much easier just to trust yourself, eyeball the pattern, and score the pieces freehand. The pieces don't have to exactly match the spaces in the pattern; close is good enough.

6 Next, using the same technique while following the pattern, fill in the flower petals by cutting and gluing slivers of rose and red-orange glass. You'll also need to fill in the bottom of the flower bud with irregular shards of green mirror nipped and shaped with glass mosaic cutters.

7 Now, using glass mosaic cutters to create small to medium, randomly shaped pieces of blue-green-yellow mix stained glass, fill in the remaining space around the blossom and down the front of the stake. Leave the bottom 6 inches (15.2 cm) of the stake—the part that will go into the ground—bare.

8 While the glue on the blossom side dries, you can cut pieces of blue mirror for the stake's edges. Using a glasscutter and running pliers, cut the blue mirror into several straight strips exactly as wide as the stake is thick, ¾ inch (1.9 cm). Then, using the glass mosaic cutters, snip two of the strips into irregular rectangles roughly ½ inch (1.3 cm) wide, laying the pieces out on your work surface in the order that they were cut.

Suzan Germond, *Wheelbarrow*, 2001,
45 x 28 inches (114 x 71 cm), metal wheelbarrow,
broken china, gems, hand-painted flower tiles.
Photo by Cal Rice.

9 Glue the pieces one after the other onto the stake's edge. Then cut one or two more strips into pieces, glue them in place, and so on until the entire edge is finished in blue mirror. At the most severe curves you'll have to snip the pieces narrower in order to keep the surface smooth. Make sure no glass sticks out over the sides. Let the glue dry completely.

TILING THE MIRROR SIDE

10 Now you're ready to work on the reverse side. I have a ring saw, so I was able to cut the large section of silver mirror for the mirror side as a single piece. To do that, put a piece of tracing paper over the mirror shape on the pattern and trace around it with pencil. Then cut out this paper shape and trace around it on the sheet of silver mirror with a permanent marker. Using a ring saw, cut the shape out and glue it in place on the garden stake. (Put the stake blossom-side down on a towel or cushion to protect it.) If you don't have access to a ring saw, you may be able to find a commercial glass dealer or stained-glass shop that can do the job for you. If not, you'll have to cut and glue the mirror in large sections. Use the glasscutter and running pliers to cut several large pieces, shape them with glass mosaic cutters, then glue the pieces in place.

11 Once you've glued the mirror section in place, finish tiling the garden stake by filling the rest of the side with blue-green-yellow mix stained glass, down to the bottom 6 inches (15.2 cm), just as you did the other side. Make sure no pieces extend over an edge. Let your work dry overnight.

GROUTING

12 Use cleaning tools to carefully remove any dried adhesive from the surface of the glass and mirror on both sides and the edges.

13 Mix the grout, colorant, and fortifier in one container and fill another with water for cleaning. Grout the blossom side and edges, pressing the material into all the spaces and using your fingers to create smooth grout lines along the edges (see page 52). Wipe away excess grout with a damp sponge, let the glass and mirror haze over, then polish the surface with a soft cloth. Cover the grout container tightly with plastic and keep it in a cool place while you let the stake's grouted side dry for 45 minutes to an hour—enough to allow turning the stake to work on the other side. Then carefully turn the stake over and grout, clean, and polish the mirror side. Wrap the stake in plastic or kraft paper and let the grout cure for three days.

Pebble Mosaic Flowerpot

Think of this beautiful, pebble-studded flowerpot as a rock garden of a different sort. Natural pebbles add rich texture; contrasting colors highlight the spiral design. You can adapt this method to almost any size or shape of flowerpot.

Materials

Ceramic flowerpot, approximately
    8 inches (20.3 cm) tall
3 pounds (1.4 kg) of mixed dark
    (black-brown-grey) pebbles
2 pounds (910 g) of light turquoise
    pebbles
Silicone glue
Polyurethane spray
2 pounds (910 g) of gray
    sanded grout
Acrylic grout fortifier

Tools and Supplies

Pattern for Pebble Mosaic
    Flowerpot (page 138)
Scissors
Tape
Ruler
Pencil
Permanent marker
Old towel or cushion
Basic Mosaic Supply Kit (page 22)

Instructions

FIGURE 1

1 Make two photocopies of the spiral pattern on page 138, enlarging the pattern to full size as indicated, and cut around the outlines with scissors.

2 Hold one of the cutout spirals up to the flowerpot and align the bottom of the pattern with the bottom of the flowerpot. Flatten the paper as much as possible and tape the pattern in place.

3 Measure exactly 2 ½ inches (6.4 cm) to the right of the taped pattern's right-most point (indicated by an X on the pattern) and make a mark on the flowerpot. Position the left-hand edge of the second spiral on this mark, again aligning the bottom of the pattern with the flowerpot's bottom, and tape the pattern down. There should now be an even distance between the two patterns on each side.

4 Trace around both patterns as best you can with a per-mament marker. Remove the tape and paper and fill in any blank areas in the traced outlines where tape or uneven paper made tracing difficult.

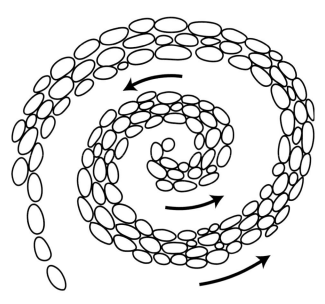

The direction of pebbles should follow the direction of the spiral.

APPLYING THE PEBBLES

5 Spread out all the dark pebbles and sort them by size and appearance, putting the nicest, flattest, most uniform large, medium, and small pebbles on separate plates. Do the same with the turquoise pebbles.

6 Put the flowerpot on its side, with one of the spiral patterns facing up, on top of a towel or cushion to hold the flowerpot steady. Using a craft stick, spread glue on about a third of the spiral, starting at its inner, or closed, end. (Make sure you're working on the spiral pattern and not the background.)

7 Using the nicest large and medium turquoise pebbles, fill in the glued area, positioning the pebbles in the direction of the spiral's flow. In other words,

orient the pebbles with their longest sides pointing in the direction of the spiral, rather than across (see figure 1).

8 Finish tiling the spiral pattern, spreading glue and positioning pebbles a section at a time.

9 Now fill in the background behind the spiral with dark pebbles. Place the dark pebbles enclosed within the turquoise spiral in the direction of the spiral. The remaining dark pebbles can be placed in any direction. Just be sure to fit them together nicely, leaving as little gap between the pebbles as possible.

When you've finished filling in as much area as you can without turning the flowerpot, let the glue dry completely.

10 Turn the pot so the second spiral pattern is facing you. Fill in this spiral and its background just as you did the first. Let the glue dry completely.

11 Fill in any remaining portions of the flowerpot's sides. Let the glue dry.

12 Set the pot upright and glue dark pebbles around the flowerpot's upper body, up to the neck. You'll work on the neck itself later.

13 Sort through the small turquoise pebbles and pick out the most perfectly oval, tiniest—about ⅔ inch (1.7 cm) long—specimens. You'll need enough to place around the top of the lip. Spread glue on the lip, then carefully position the little pebbles end to end, keeping them in perfect alignment in a centered row all around the lip's surface. Let the glue dry.

14 Now you're ready to work on the inside of the lip. Again, sort through the small turquoise pebbles and pick out the tiniest ones. These don't have to be perfectly shaped, though. Spread the glue carefully around the inside lip and fill in the area with three or four rows of little pebbles. Let the glue dry.

15 Next, turn the flowerpot back on its side on a towel or cushion so you can work on the neck. Fill the band around the neck with small dark pebbles, taking care as you work not to slop glue on the pebbles already in place on either side. Make sure none of the pebbles extends up over the edge of the lip. Let the flowerpot dry overnight.

GROUTING

16 Use cleaning tools to remove any adhesive dried on the surface of the pebbles—be careful, though, not to scratch the pebbles. Then, either outdoors or in a well-ventilated area, lightly spray the pebbles with polyurethane. Use just enough to coat them so the grout won't permanently adhere to the pebbles, but not enough to make them look glossy. Let the polyurethane dry completely.

17 Mix the grout and fortifier to the desired consistency. You'll grout the flowerpot in sections, starting with the lip and neck. Make sure to push the grout firmly into all the spaces around the pebbles. Take care to grout the inside of the lip as well as the top, and to create smooth edges around the lip.

18 Now, while you let the grout on the lip and neck partially set, you can start grouting the main body. Grout about a third of the body, again carefully filling all the spaces around all the pebbles. Then go back to the lip and neck and, with a damp sponge, wipe away excess grout from that area.

19 Grout another third of the flowerpot's body; then, while that section partially sets, wipe away excess grout from the preceding section with a damp sponge—and so on until you've grouted and sponged the entire flowerpot.

If at some point in the process a pebble falls off, dry that area thoroughly, add new adhesive and replace the pebble. Let the glue dry while you work on the rest of the pot, then re-grout that pebble and sponge it clean.

20 When the grouted pebbles have hazed over, polish them briskly with a soft cloth until they're clean. Wrap the flowerpot in plastic or kraft paper and let the grout cure for three days.

Virginia Bullman, *Sheep Pothead Pair* (photos above; detail, top), 1999, 24 x 16 x 18 inches (61 x 40.6 x 45.7 cm), pebble mosaic on ceramic thimble and flower pot. Photo by Hank Margeson.

Mosaic Accent Bricks

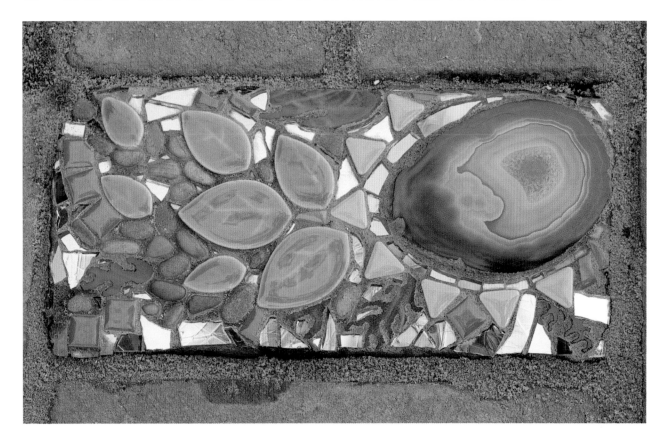

There's no place like home . . . especially when you've added creative personal touches, such as your own mosaic brick road. Because a design for a single brick needs only a little of this and a little of that, this project is great for utilizing materials from the scrap box.

Materials

(for one brick)

1 brick paver
1 polished agate slice, about
 ¼ x 2 x 3 inches (0.6 x 5 x 7.6 cm)
7 slate blue ceramic tile triangles,
 ½ inch (1.3 cm) wide
7 leaf-shaped blue ceramic tiles
 (2 large, 2 medium, and 3 small)
6 dark teal ceramic tiles, ⅜ inch
 (9.5 mm) square

1 handful of ¼- to ½-inch (0.6 to
 1.3 cm) turquoise/teal pebbles
1 3 x 3-inch (7.6 x 7.6 cm) piece
 of blue/white ring mottled
 stained glass
1 1 x 1-½-inch (2.5 x 3.8 cm) piece
 of light blue mirror
1 3 x 3-inch (7.6 x 7.6 cm) piece of
 blue with white mix stained glass
Waterproof glue
¼ pound (113 g) of blue
 sanded grout
Acrylic grout fortifier

Tools and Supplies

Pattern for Mosaic Accent Brick
 (page 139)
Basic Mosaic Supply Kit
 (page 22)

Note: I've provided just one brick pattern, but I hope you'll have fun creating several of these miniature mosaics, varying the designs. If you're planning to make enough bricks to add to a patio or pathway, remember that although each brick is its own composition, they all must somehow work together. What will be the unifying factor in your group of bricks? Will you use similar materials in each? Will you use repeating design elements, or will the family of color unite your bricks?

Instructions

1 Use the pattern on page 139 as a rough guideline for positioning the pieces. With the brick paver positioned vertically in front of you, start by placing the agate on the brick, angling the agate slightly inward from the lower right corner to establish movement. When you're happy with its position, lift the agate slightly, brush glue onto that area of the paver, and push the agate onto the glue with gentle, firm pressure.

2 Paint glue around the agate's outside edge and place the ceramic tile triangles next, positioning them so they radiate outward, as if the agate was a sun.

3 Use glass mosaic cutters to nip small, mostly rectangular shapes of blue and white ring mottled glass. Glue them between the agate and ceramic triangles.

4 Glue the leaf-shaped ceramic tiles in place, with the smallest curving off gently to the right at the top. Then position and glue the six dark teal tiles.

5 Use the small teal and turquoise pebbles to fill in between the leaves. Put a few outside of the leaves, too. Take advantage of their shapes by placing them so they flow in the same direction as the leaves.

6 Fill in the rest of the space on the brick with small shards of blue with white mix stained glass, adding bits of blue mirror here and there as accents. Let the glue dry overnight.

7 Remove any dried glue from the surface of the glass, agate, and mirror.

8 Mix the grout and additive, then grout the brick's surface and outside edge. Wipe with a damp sponge, let the surface haze over, and polish with a soft cloth. Use cleaning tools to remove any dried grout remnants. Wrap the brick and let cure for three days.

9 Place the mosaicked brick, and others if you've made them, among ordinary bricks in a loose-laid patio or walkway (one in sand or earth). Set the mosaicked bricks deep enough to make their surfaces level with the others.

Agate Candle Lantern

Textured glass and thin slices of natural agate add even more warmth and charm to candlelight's golden glow. Start with a lantern like the one in the photo or apply the same techniques to a different lamp of your choosing.

Materials

Metal and glass candle lantern with stand (see Note, next page)
8 to 10 3-inch (7.6 cm) polished agate slices
3 6 x 6-inch (15.2 x 15.2 cm) or larger pieces of textured clear glass, each a different texture
Silicone glue
Masking tape
1 ½ pounds (681g) of black sanded grout
Acrylic grout fortifier
Candle

Tools and Supplies

Towel or cushion
Glass mosaic cutters
Basic Mosaic Supply Kit
(page 22)

Jan Hinson, *Poodle Settee,* **1999,**
46 x 66 inches (117 x 168 cm), lightweight
ferro-cement forms, reset broken tile.
Photo by artist.

Instructions

Note: This is probably the easiest project in the book, and also one of the most enjoyable. The toughest part may be finding a lantern and stand that you like. "Coachman" style lanterns like the one I used are widely available in home-supply stores—or you may prefer some other type with clear, flat panes. In any case, look for models with real glass panes, not plastic.

1 Lay the lantern on its side on a cushion or folded towel. Glue one, two, or even three agates onto one of the lantern's panes, placing them more or less randomly.

2 Using the glass mosaic cutters, nip the textured glass into a variety of shapes and sizes. You don't have to cut all the glass at once; just cut enough of each texture to get you started on the pane, then nip off more as needed. Keep the different textures separated in different piles. Glue pieces onto the lantern, filling in around the agates while leaving about ⅛ inch (3 mm) of space between the pieces for grout. Vary the textures and mix small pieces with some larger for contrast. Let this side dry for about 15 minutes.

3 Working one side at a time, as in the preceding steps, glue the agates and textured glass to the remaining panes. Vary the placement and number of agates, and the positions, sizes, and textures of glass pieces, to create visual variety. Let the four sides dry overnight.

4 Cover all the metal parts adjacent to the lantern's panes with masking tape, to keep them clean of grout. Be sure to press the tape down smooth and tight.

5 Mix the grout and fortifier in one container and fill another with water for cleanup.

6 Set the lantern upright and, with gloved hands, carefully spread the grout, forcing it down into all the crevices around the glass and agates. Grout all four sides to the point where each has been wiped with a damp sponge to remove excess. By the time you finish grouting the fourth side, the first will have had enough time to dry and haze over. Polish with a soft cloth. Use a razor blade and/or dental tools to remove stubborn spots on the agates or textured glass. Repeat with the other three sides.

7 Wrap the lamp in plastic or kraft paper and let the grout cure for three days.

8 Install the candle.

Cleo Mussi, *Chomondely Cats,* **1999,**
39 ½ x 11 ¾ x 15 ¾ inches (100.3 x 30 x 40 cm),
metal substructure, recycled china. Photo by artist.

Ceramic Tile Plant Surround

Bold geometric patterns and strong, rambling grout lines merge in this eye-catching base designed to highlight a favorite plant. I used hand-painted Mexican tiles that I found bargain-priced on an Internet auction site.

Materials

Materials for plant surround base
  (page 29)
5 green decorative 4 x 4-inch
  (10.2 x 10.2 cm) glazed ceramic tiles
7 dark green 4 x 4-inch
  (10.2 x 10.2 cm) glazed ceramic tiles
15 to 16 light green 4 x 4-inch
  (10.2 x 10.2 cm) glazed ceramic tiles
Silicone glue
2 ½ pounds (1.1 kg) blue sanded grout
1 ounce (30 mL) yellow liquid pure
  pigment
Acrylic grout fortifier

Tools and Supplies

Tools for plant surround base
  (page 29)
Pattern for Ceramic Tile Plant
  Surround (page 140)
Ceramic tile cutter
Ceramic tile nippers
Hammer
Leather gloves
Basic Mosaic Supply Kit (page 22)

Instructions

BASE CONSTRUCTION

1 Make the plant surround base following the instructions on pages 29 through 31.

TILING

2 Using the tile cutter, cut one decorative tile (tile A on the pattern) in half diagonally. You'll use one half, and a corner portion from the other half, along the base's bottom edge.

3 For the tile placed along the inner circle (tile B) use tile nippers to nip a curve into one corner that will align with the inner circle's curve.

4 Next break all the decorative tiles (including the nipped tile B and the two tile A halves) into pieces one at a time. To do this, hold the tile face down in a gloved hand, as shown on page 18, and strike the tile's back with a hammer. Then use tile nippers to nip the tile's large pieces into smaller ones. As you break up each tile be sure to reassemble the pieces on your work surface to keep from mixing them up with other tiles.

5 Now you're ready to place the tiles. (You don't have to transfer the pattern to the cone for this project; just use it as a guide for eyeballing the tile positions.) With a craft stick, spread a layer of glue on the base the size of the decorative tile you'll be laying. Then carefully press the pieces into position, leaving $1/16$ to $1/8$ inch (1.6 to 3 mm) of space

between them, recreating each tile or portion of tile as shown on the pattern. As you work you may have to nip some pieces into smaller pieces to keep the curving surface smooth, with no jagged edges sticking up. Be sure, too, to keep the tiles along the inside and outside edges flush to the edge; don't let them extend over.

6 With all the decorative tiles positioned, you can create their borders. Use the tile cutter to slice the dark green tiles into $1/2$-inch (1.3 cm) strips. You'll probably be able to get only about five strips per tile before the piece gets too small to hold onto and cut.

7 Next, using your nippers, nip each strip into $1/2$-inch-long (1.3 cm) pieces, cutting on the diagonal. As you cut them lay out the pieces in order, fitting them almost back together. This makes gluing the pieces on the base much easier and faster. Go ahead and do just that: Glue the strips of dark green around the outside edges of each of the decorative tiles.

8 Now break and nip the light green tiles into pieces, and use them to fill in the spaces

remaining between the bordered decorative tiles. Again, remember to place edge pieces flush to the edge, and when necessary cut large pieces smaller to keep them from sticking up and to maintain a smooth surface. Let the surround dry overnight.

GROUTING

9 Following the instructions on page 51, mix the yellow and green colorants into the dry grout and stir in 3 to 4 ounces (90 to 120 mL) of fortifier. Add more colorant if necessary until the color matches the dark border tiles. Then mix in enough additional fortifier to give the grout the desired consistency.

10 Grout the cone, taking particular care to create a smooth and even-looking grout line at the lower and upper edges. Sponge off extra grout, let the surface dry for 15 minutes, and then polish. Use cleaning tools to remove any remaining unwanted grout. Wrap the surround in plastic or kraft paper and cure for three days.

Ashley's Fancy Frogs

Using storebought ceramic frogs, my daughter made these playful, ornate amphibians as gifts for friends. The instructions here are for the large frog sitting on a lily pad. Adjust the materials quantities accordingly for the frog you use. The procedure will be about the same—except that if your frog doesn't have a base you won't have to do as much grouting and masking.

Materials

Porcelain frog, approximately
   5 inches (12.7 cm) tall

Stained glass:
4 x 4-inch (10.2 x 10.2 cm) piece
   of green stained glass
5 x 5-inch (12.7 x 12.7 cm) piece
   of yellow stained glass
6 x 6-inch (15.2 x 15.2 cm) piece
   of orange stained glass
6 x 6-inch (15.2 x 15.2 cm) piece
   of iridescent red stained glass

4 x 4-inch (10.2 x 10.2 cm) piece
   of silver mirror
Multipurpose waterproof glue
1 1/2 pounds (681 g) of white
   sanded grout
1/2 ounce (15 mL) of light green
   liquid pure pigment
1/4 ounce (7.5 mL) of yellow liquid
   pure pigment
1 ounce (30 mL) of red liquid
   pure pigment
3/4 ounce (22.5 mL) orange liquid
   pure pigment
Acrylic grout fortifier

Tools and Supplies

Tile-Making Kit (page 19)
Glass mosaic cutters
Permanent marker
Inexpensive hobby paintbrush
Scissors
Masking tape
Basic Mosaic Supply Kit (page 22)

Instructions

1 Following the instructions on
   page 19, cut all the stained
glass and mirror into 1/4-inch-
wide (6 mm) strips. Cutting
strips this thin can be difficult;
just do your best to cut them as
small as you can. Then use glass
mosaic cutters to nip the strips
into tiny squareish tesserae. Keep
each color on its own paper plate.

2 Using the frogs in the photo
   as guides, draw narrow swirls—
where you'll be placing mirror—on
the frog's front and back with the
permanent marker. The design
and number of swirls is up to you.
On the red frog there are three
rows of mirror swirls coming up
from below on its tummy and
three rows on its back, plus a small
swirl creeping up each front leg.

3 Now carefully tile each swirl
   with a single row of miniature mirror pieces: Apply glue
along a section of a swirl line.
Then, using glass mosaic cutters,
nip and shape the tiles for that
section and place them end to
end in the direction of the swirl's
movement. Because the tesserae
for this project are so small,
you'll probably need to use
tweezers for all the tiling.

4 Once you've tiled all the
   mirrored swirls, you're ready
to fill in the larger areas. Start
with the lily pad base (if your
frog has one). Brush glue on one
small section at a time, approximately 2 x 2 inches (5 x 5 cm).
Then tile the section with random shards of green stained
glass. Be careful not to cover the
frog's front or back feet, though.

5 Now tile the lower third of
   the frog in red stained glass,
cutting and shaping the glass tiles
where needed to fill in around
the mirror swirls. Tile whatever
portion of the frog's legs are in
the lower third, too. Because
you're tiling a vertical surface it's
important to start from the bottom up, allowing the glue to dry
a minute or two as you work so
that each row supports the one
you place above it.

6 Tile the middle third of the
   frog next, using orange
stained glass. Again, nip the
pieces as necessary to fit around
the swirls.

7 Tile the top third of the frog
   in yellow stained glass. In
order to keep the mosaicked surface even along the rounded contours of the frog's head and face,
you'll have to snip the tesserae
into teensy pieces and use tweezers to place them. Don't tile the
eyes; leave a gap approximately
1/8 inch (3 mm) around the eye,
to provide space for grouting.
When you've finished tiling, let
the glue dry overnight.

GROUTING

8 Carefully clean away any dried glue from the surface of the glass and mirror. Now mask off the eyes. Using scissors, cut from tape two circles exactly the same size and shape as the eyes and stick them on, smoothing the edges. Make sure the tape circles are no larger than the eyes, so that when you remove the tape after grouting the grout won't pull away too.

9 If your frog doesn't have a lily pad base, proceed to step 11. Otherwise, you'll need to grout the lily pad first. Mask off the lower third of the frog's body, including its toes and legs. Make a nice clean edge where the body and feet meet the lily pad, smoothing the tape down firmly. Mix ½ pound (227 g) of the grout with the light green and yellow pigments and acrylic grout fortifier. Then, while wearing gloves, work the grout into all the spaces and along the lily pad's outside edge, remembering to grout along the underside too. Wrap the frog in plastic or kraft paper and let the green grout set up overnight.

10 Carefully remove the masking tape from the lower third of the frog's body. Then, using small pieces of tape, mask off the area along the grouted lily pad where it meets the frog's body and legs.

11 Mix 1 pound (454 g) of grout with the red and orange pigments and grout fortifier. It should be a deep red-orange, a color that will make the different colors of stained glass blend together. Grout the frog, filling all the spaces with even pressure. Wipe off the excess grout using a damp sponge. Let the surface glaze over, then polish it with a soft cloth. Carefully remove the masking tape from the eyes. Remove any stubborn dried grout with cleaning tools. Wrap the frog in plastic or kraft paper and let it cure for three days.

Craigie, *Mo the Turtle*, 2001,
5 x 4 feet x 10 inches (1.5 x 1.2 m x 25.4 cm), stained glass, ceramic tile, agates on cement base. Photo by Evan Bracken.

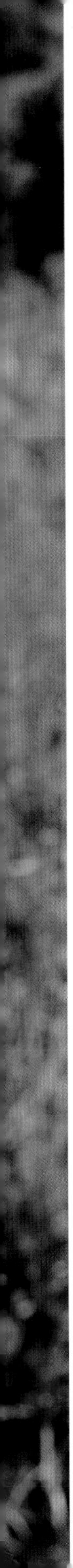

Onion Dome Birdhouse

This is the Taj Mahal of birdhouses, a veritable feathered-friend palace crowned by a brilliant gold-leaf dome. Despite its luxury, the birdhouse has a practical side, too: its body detaches from the base for easy seasonal cleaning. Of course, palaces aren't built in a day; allow plenty of time to build and mosaic this majestic structure.

Materials

Exterior grade plywood, ¾ inch (1.9 cm), or other rot-resistant wood

Sandpaper, medium and coarse grits

Wood glue

1 ¼-inch (3.2 cm) finish nails

Wooden ball finial, 4 inches (10.2 cm) in diameter with flared base

1 pound (454 g) of polymer sculpturing compound

Wood sealer

Epoxy glue in syringe

Metallic gold enamel paint

⅜ x 1-inch (9.5 mm x 2.5 cm) flathead wood screws

Materials for making gold-leaf glass (page 14)

⅜ x ⅜-inch (9.5 x 9.5 mm) ceramic tiles in the following quantities and colors:

¼ pound (113g) each of dark teal, deep brown

½ pound (227 g) each of black, metallic gold

1 ½ pounds (681 g) teal blend (mixed light, medium, dark teal tiles)

1 pound (454 g) ceramic tile leaf shapes, assorted sizes ¾ to 1 ¼ inches (1.9 to 3.2 cm); blues, greens, goldenrod

Silicone glue

1 pound (454 g) of white sanded grout

¼ ounce (7.5 mL) of yellow liquid pure pigment

4 to 5 drops of yellow ochre liquid pure pigment

3 ½ pounds (1.6 kg) of black sanded grout

Acrylic grout fortifier

Dowel rod, ¼-inch (6 mm) diameter

Tools and Supplies

Pattern for Onion Dome
    Birdhouse (pages 141 to 143)
Pattern Transfer Kit (page 42)
Circular, table, or hand saw
Ruler
Hammer
Jigsaw
Electric drill with bits
Paintbrush
Baking sheet
Lazy Susan (optional but
    recommended)
Glass mosaic cutters
Old towel or cushion
Tile nippers
Clay cleanup tool
Basic Mosaic Supply Kit
    (page 22)

**Sherri Warner Hunter, St. Andrew's
Sewanee Totem Series (detail), 2001,**
72 to 90 inches tall (1.8 x 2.3 m),
10 to 25 inches wide (25 x 63.5 cm) concrete
forms, ceramic, glass. Photo by artist.

Instructions

CONSTRUCTING THE BIRDHOUSE

1 Saw the wood into the seven
    section pieces on the cutting
list below. Sand all the surfaces
and edges smooth, starting with
coarse-grit sandpaper and finishing with medium-grit.

2 Using a ruler and pencil
    measure and mark a line 1 5/8
inches (4.1 cm) in from each edge
of the base board. Spread wood
glue on one side of the base
bracket and place the bracket on
the base board, centered within
the marked lines. Nail the bracket
in place with a finish nail at each
of the bracket's four corners.

3 Transfer the patterns for the
    front and side sections onto
their respective pieces. Go over
the lines with permanent marker.

4 Drill a 3/8-inch (9.5 mm)
    pilot hole into the doorway
area of the front board. Then use
a jigsaw to cut out the doorway
opening. Drill a 3/16-inch (5 mm)
hole for the perch, positioned as
shown on the pattern.

5 Now glue and nail the four
    walls together, with the smaller
side boards positioned between the
larger front and back boards. Be
sure you've placed the side boards
so the right and left patterns are
facing in the right directions.

6 Glue and nail the top board
    centered over the square shell
of the birdhouse. When the top is
properly positioned, 1/4 inch (6
mm) of the top edge of all four
walls will show around the top
board's perimeter. (See
figure 1 for an exploded view
of the birdhouse assembly.)

Cutting List For Birdhouse Sections

Code	Description	Qty	Dimensions
A	Front	1	4 5/8" x 7" (11.8 x 17.8 cm)
B	Back	1	4 5/8" x 7" (11.8 x 17.8 cm)
C	Sides	2	3 1/8" x 7" (7.9 x 17.8 cm)
D	Base	1	6 1/2" x 6 1/2" (16.5 x 16.5 cm)
E	Base Bracket	1	3 1/8" x 3 1/8" (7.9 x 7.9 cm)
F	Top	1	4 1/4" x 4 1/4" (10.8 x 10.8 cm)

FIGURE 1

Birdhouse Assembly
Exploded View

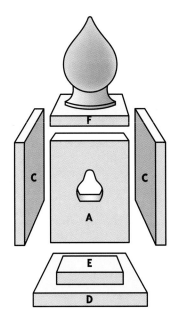

FIGURE 2

Building up Finial with Sculpturing Compound to Create Onion Dome

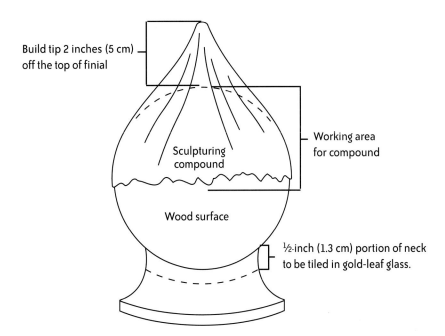

Build tip 2 inches (5 cm) off the top of finial

Sculpturing compound

Working area for compound

Wood surface

½-inch (1.3 cm) portion of neck to be tiled in gold-leaf glass.

ADDING THE DOME

7 Now it's time to sculpt a tip onto the ball finial, creating an onion dome shape. Knead and press pieces of sculpturing compound onto the finial, smoothing it as you go, working upward from the "equator." Build the material up around the finial gradually, increasing the thickness from very thin at the middle to a rounded point that rises 2 inches (5 cm) above the top of the ball, as shown in figure 2. Turn the finial frequently as you work, checking from various angles to make sure the dome is symmetrical. If your finial's base has ridges, fill in and smooth the ridges with compound after you've sculpted the dome. The entire surface needs to be smooth to accommodate tiling.

8 Read the instructions and precautions on page 28 for baking polymer. Put the modified finial on a baking sheet on the center rack in an oven preheated to 225° F (126° C). Bake for approximately 45 minutes in a well-ventilated room, checking after 30 minutes to make sure the clay isn't burning. Remove the finial from the oven after it has cooled.

9 Spread epoxy glue on the finial's base and center the dome on top of the birdhouse. Let the glue dry completely.

10 Brush wood sealer onto the onion dome and exterior of all the birdhouse components, including the base. Make sure to cover the edges thoroughly. Apply a second coat after the first has dried.

11 Slip the bottom of the birdhouse over the base bracket and onto the base. Drill a ⅛-inch (3 mm) diameter hole centered ¼ inch (6 mm) up from the bottom of one side board, boring through the side board and into the bracket. Do the same on the other side. Then sink a wood screw into each of the two holes. This will allow you to remove the birdhouse from its base each year to clean out last year's nest.

TILING THE DOME AND DOORWAY

12 Paint the dome and the upper ½ inch (1.3 cm) of the neck with metallic gold enamel paint. Paint the doorway area with gold enamel, too (see the pattern).

13 Follow the directions on page 14 for making gold-leaf glass. You'll need to make at least two 5 x 5-inch (12.7 x 12.7 cm) sheets. Then use glass mosaic cutters to nip the glass (foil-side up to minimize scratching the gold leaf) into small irregular shards.

14 Now you're ready to tile the dome. Start at the base of the ball, not the neck, and work around the ball and upward, spreading glue and cutting and positioning pieces on one small area at a time. Make sure the glass shards are small enough to allow you to keep the surface smooth despite the ball's rounded contour. You'll have to snip the glass into especially tiny pieces and use tweezers to place them when tiling the dome's top and tip. When you've finished the dome itself, glue gold leaf shards around the painted upper ½ inch (1.3 cm) of the neck, where it meets the ball. Let the glue dry completely.

15 Carefully place the birdhouse on its back, supported by a towel or cushion. Again using shards of gold-leaf glass nipped and shaped to fit, tile the painted area around the doorway, as indicated on the pattern.

TILING THE BIRDHOUSE BODY

16 Next, use tile nippers to nip 10 black tiles into halves. Glue the halves in a row on the top board's (piece F) front-facing edge, along the bottom. Position each tile's cut side facing down and the opposite smooth side facing up. Then glue mixed-color teal tiles in a row above the black tile pieces, flush to the top of the wood's edge (use the photos for reference).

17 Now it's time to concentrate on tiling the rest of the front. Glue a row of whole metallic gold tiles along the bottom. For the top row, place a single black tile in the middle, put one whole metallic gold tile on each side of the black tile, then fill in the remainder of the row with metallic gold tiles cut into thirds. Be sure to position the rough cut edges facing down, so only the smooth uncut edges of the tiles face up.

18 Next, glue the green leaves in place. Then use black tiles to fill the space around the doorway and leaves. This is also the time to glue three whole black tiles above the bottom row of gold tiles, as shown on the pattern. Add one metallic gold tile at each corner of the doorway, and nip a third into two small triangles, one straddling either side of the lowest leaf.

19 With all the detail work completed, fill in the rest of the front with dark teal tiles. Keep the tiles whole except where you have to nip and shape them around the doorway's decorative trim. Let the entire front side dry for at least 45 minutes, then carefully turn the birdhouse so that one of its sides is facing up.

20 Tile the top board's edge on this side using the same materials and procedure described in step 16.

21 Glue a row of whole metallic gold tiles across the side board's bottom, taking care not to tile over the screw. Then cut and glue a row of one-third-size metallic gold tiles across the top, much as you did in step 17.

22 Now, following the pattern and color chart, fill in the details, tiling the brown vine first and then adding the leaves.

23 Finally, tile the background with mixed teal, varying the placement of the light, medium, and dark hues and using whole tiles as much as possible. Nip the tiles where necessary to shape them around the vine and leaves.

24 Let the glue on the tiled side dry for at least 45 minutes. Then carefully turn the birdhouse so the back is facing up.

25 Tile the top board's edge on the back side using the same materials and procedure described in step 16.

26 Repeat step 21, adding a thin strip of metallic gold at the back's upper facing edge and a whole-tile strip along the lower facing edge.

27 Fill the remainder of the back with mixed teal, again varying the placement of the hues and using whole tiles as much as possible. Let the glue dry for at least 45 minutes before turning the birdhouse to the remaining untiled side.

28 Repeat steps 20 through 23. When you've finished tiling the last side, let the glue dry for at least 45 minutes before turning the birdhouse upright. Put the birdhouse on a lazy Susan if you have one.

TILING THE BASE

29 Now you're ready to tile the base. Use the photo on page 74 as a guide. Line the base's edge with two rows of black tiles—one row of whole tiles along the top portion of the edge, and a row cut to about two-thirds width to fit along the bottom. Make sure the cut sides are facing down.

30 On the top surface of the base board, glue a metallic gold tile in each corner, then put a black tile on each of the open sides next to it. Cut another metallic gold tile to fit, if necessary, in the space flanking the two black tiles. Then fill in the remainder of the base with dark teal tile, using whole tiles as much as possible. Just be sure to leave a $1/16$-inch (1.6 mm) space along the inner edge on all four sides, where the base meets the birdhouse's walls, so you'll be able to take the birdhouse apart for cleaning. Position the tiles on these inner rows with their cut sides facing toward the wall.

31 To finish your birdhouse, glue a row of whole metallic gold tiles around the dome's base. Then fill the untiled gap between the metallic gold tile and gold-leaf shards with a row of black tile, cutting them to whatever width is necessary. Congratulations; you're finished tiling! Let the glue dry overnight.

GROUTING

32 Carefully use a razor blade and dental picks to remove any dried glue from the surface of the tile and glass.

33 You'll be grouting the gold-leaf areas—the onion dome and doorway trim—first. Using masking tape, mask off the ceramic tile under the dome, on the neck. Also mask off the ceramic tiles that border the gold-leaf section of the doorway. After masking off around the door, cover the entire body of the birdhouse—everything below the dome—with plastic sheeting secured in place with tape.

Jo Letchford, Cockerel & Co., 2001, pre-cast concrete ornament, ceramic tiles, vitreous glass, aquarium gravel. Photo by Colin Bowling.

34 Mix the white grout, pigments, and acrylic fortifier and carefully grout the dome and the portion of the neck tiled in gold-leaf shards. Wipe off excess grout with a damp sponge, allow the surface to haze over, then polish it with a soft cloth.

35 Unwrap enough of the body to give you access to the doorway trim, and grout that section of gold-leaf glass. Sponge and polish the surface. Cover the section back up and let the grout set up overnight.

36 Unwrap the birdhouse and carefully peel away all the masking tape. Before you can grout the rest of the birdhouse you'll have to mask off the onion dome and doorway. Carefully run masking tape around the neck of the dome, along the lower edge of the gold-leaf glass, leaving the black and metallic gold tile exposed. Drape the rest of the dome with plastic and tape it down loosely. Now tape off the gold-leaf glass around the doorway. Cover the hole you drilled for the perch, too.

37 Unscrew and separate the birdhouse body from the base.

38 Mix the black grout and acrylic fortifier. Grout the body, focusing first on filling the joints around the top edges and the neck of the dome, and along the edges where the walls meet. Then grout the front, side, and back surfaces. Be sure to lift the body of the birdhouse and grout along the lower edge from underneath. Don't leave any lumps of grout on the underside, though, or the birdhouse won't sit level on the base.

39 Wipe away all excess grout from the birdhouse with a damp sponge. Use the clay cleanup tool to clear grout out of the screw hole on each of the two sides. Then, while you let the grout on the birdhouse haze over, grout the base. Fill all the joints along the outer edges first. Then grout the surface. Be careful not to leave too much grout along the inside edges of the tile, or you'll have trouble reassembling the birdhouse. Use a damp sponge to wipe along these inside edges and to remove excess grout from the rest of the base.

40 While the base hazes over, use cleaning tools to remove any dried grout from the birdhouse body, then polish the surface with a soft cloth. Finally, clean and polish the base.

41 Reassemble the birdhouse. Wrap it in plastic or kraft paper and let it cure for three days.

42 For my birdhouse perch, I used a piece of an old paint brush handle. But a piece of dowel rod cut 1 ½ inches (3.8 cm) long works nicely, too. Apply wood sealer and let dry; then give the dowel a coat of metallic gold enamel paint. Apply a dab of wood glue to one end of the perch. Use a hammer to lightly tap the glued end about ½ inch (1.3 cm) into the hole.

Nodding Pod Planters

Perched atop slender "stems," these diminutive glittering planters seem almost like plants themselves—though perhaps from a far-off, more whimsical world. Each will be unique because you create the pods from pinch pots you make yourself.

Materials

(for three pods)

³/₄ pound (341 g) of polymer
    sculpturing compound
5 feet (1.5 m) of ¹/₈-inch
    (3 mm) steel rod
Epoxy putty
3 or more colors of stained glass,
    6 x 6 inch (15.2 x 15.2 cm)
    pieces or larger
1 or more colors of mirror,
    6 x 6-inch (15.2 x 15.2 cm)
    pieces or larger
Silicone glue
1 pound (454 g) of sanded grout
Liquid pure pigment
Acrylic grout fortifier

Tools and Supplies

Round toothpick
Baking sheet
Wire cutters
Tile-Making Kit (page 19)
Basic Mosaic Supply Kit (page 22)

Instructions

1 Make three pod planters following the instructions on pages 38 and 39. Make sure their upper lips are flat and smooth, because you'll be laying a row of tesserae there. Before you bake them, remember to poke at least three small holes in the bottom of each for drainage. Use wire cutters to snip the steel rod into three sections of varying length—whatever heights you want your pod planters to be, plus an extra 4 to 5 inches (10.2 to 12.7 cm) for the portion of rod that will be underground when you poke it into the soil.

2 Sketch out a design on each planter with a pencil, then go over the lines with permanent marker. Remember there's precious little surface area to work with to establish a design. Start by placing a band for tiles around the top outside edge (see the photo on page 41). Then add design features such as spirals, stripes, or curves.

TILING

3 Using a glasscutter and running pliers, score and break the glass and mirror into tesserae roughly 5/16 inch (8 mm) square, following the instructions on page 19. The squares must be small to be proportionate to the pods themselves, and to lie flat on the surface. The color choice is yours. You can use a single color palette for all the pods, or make each pod a different color but repeat the same design and details. Or make every pod completely different. I included mirror on each of my pods to bring a jewel-like quality to them, and used bright, showy colors. But there's no reason why you couldn't use a muted or serious color palette for less fanciful, more distinguished pod planters.

4 Using tweezers, glue and place the tiles. Fill in the upper band and the design features first, then fill in the background behind those details. Tile the top lip and a row on the inside of the lip last. When you've finished all three pods, let them dry overnight.

GROUTING

5 Mix only a small amount of grout for each pod. Choose colors based on the colors you used for the glass and mirror. If you decide to use the same color grout for all the pods, you can just make a single batch and grout them all at once. Otherwise mix each color separately and grout the pods one at a time. In either case you'll need only a few drops of colorant. Mix it in, then add liquid fortifier sparingly.

6 Work the grout into the spaces between the tesserae. Pay particular attention to the area where the wire meets the pod and to the lip's inner and outer edges. Use your fingertips to smooth those edges nicely. Even if you grout all three pods at once there's so little surface area you should have no trouble with the grout setting up before you can get back to clean it. Remove excess with a damp sponge, allow the tiles to haze over, and then polish with a soft cloth. Re-poke the drain holes carefully if they became clogged during grouting and cleaning.

7 Wrap each pod in plastic or kraft paper and let cure for three days.

Not Your Ordinary House Number

If you want to communicate not only where you live but also the creative spirit that lives within, identify your location with this number that says you're anything but a number. Use the numeral templates on page 145 to adapt this project to your address.

Materials

(see Note on next page)

12 x 36-inch (30.5 x 91.5 cm) piece of ³⁄₄-inch (1.9 cm) rot-resistant wood

Medium-grit sandpaper

Wood glue

4 1-inch (2.5 cm) finish nails

Wood sealer

4 x 4-inch (10.2 x 10.2 cm) ceramic tiles in the following quantities and colors:
2 each of slate blue, orange
3 each of red, kelly green
4 of royal blue
6 each of black, mustard yellow

6 x 6-inch (15.2 x 15.2 cm) piece of yellow mirror

12 x 12-inch (30.5 x 30.5 cm) sheet of silver mirror

Silicone glue

1 ¹⁄₂ pounds (681 g) of blue sanded grout

³⁄₄ ounce (22.5 mL) of phthalo blue liquid pure pigment

1 ¹⁄₂ pounds (681 g) of white sanded grout

1 ¹⁄₂ ounces (45 mL) of yellow liquid pure pigment

Acrylic grout fortifier

Tools and Supplies

Pattern for House Number
  (page 144)
Pattern Transfer Kit (page 42)
Jigsaw or scroll saw
Hammer
Paintbrush
Leather gloves
Ceramic tile nippers
Tile-Making Kit (page 19)
Glass mosaic cutters
Basic Mosaic Supply Kit (page 22)

Candace Bahouth, *Blue Wall,* **1998,** stone wall, broken china. Photo by Debbie Patterson.

Instructions

Note: If your house number includes more than three digits either reduce the size of the numbers to fit within the space or make the entire project proportionately larger. If your house number has only one or two digits, consider filling the extra space on either side with a decorative tile or design.

1 Transfer the designs for the starburst back board and the arched number area front board separately onto the wood (see Transferring Patterns, page 41). To do this, first trace around the pattern's entire outer perimeter, transferring the starburst back board's shape. Then, on a separate section of the wood, transfer the outline and design for the arched number area (delineated by dotted lines on the pattern). Throughout the instructions I'll refer to the small arched board as the front board and the large starburst as the back board.

2 Carefully cut out both pieces using a jigsaw or scroll saw (if you don't have either, take the job to a woodworking shop). Smooth any rough edges with sandpaper.

3 Glue and nail the front board in place on top of the back board. Let the glue dry thoroughly before proceeding to the next step.

4 After using a photocopier to enlarge them as needed, transfer your house numbers onto the front board. Simply cut the properly sized numbers from the photocopy paper with scissors, position them on the board, and trace around each with a permanent marker.

5 Apply two coats of outdoor wood sealer to the wood both front and back, allowing drying time between coats. (You may have to do just one side and the edges first, then the other side.) Let the sealer dry completely overnight.

TILING

6 Wearing leather gloves and using a hammer, break up three to four black tiles (see page 18). Use tile nippers to cut and shape the pieces into smaller shards and glue them to fill the back board's rays.

7 To fashion the triangular shapes that border the numbers on the front board, use a hammer to break up the red and orange ceramic tiles, and then use tile nippers to shape and size the triangles. As you can see from the photo, the triangles don't have to be perfectly shaped, or exactly the same shape and size as those in the pattern. Just use the pattern as a guide to the triangles' relative sizes and alternating colors as you glue them in place. Do make sure, however, that none of the triangles is tall enough to touch the front board's top edge, so that you'll have enough room for the blue border.

8 Next, break up the kelly green tiles and, using tile nippers and gluing the pieces in place as you work, fit green triangles between the red and orange ones. Again, leave plenty of room for the blue border; the green triangles' bases can be below the tips of the red and orange triangles.

9 Now it's time to tile the curved blue border. Break two blue tiles into large pieces, then use tile nippers to fashion strips, each cut to fit between a given pair of red and orange triangles. The distance between the tips of the red and orange triangles determines the length of the piece you need to cut. The width of the border should range from $1/2$ to $5/8$ inch (1.3 to 1.6 cm). Make the lengthwise cut first, using the nippers to produce a slight curve. Then cut the strip widthwise, angling each end to match the angles of the red and orange triangle tips the strip will fit between. Glue each strip in place as you cut it.

10 Set the tile cutter at $1/2$ inch (1.3 cm) and cut one black tile into strips. Then use tile nippers to cut the strip at angles into smaller pieces. Glue them across the bottom edge, creating a black border under the numbers.

11 Next break, nip, and glue shards of royal blue tiles to fill the numbers. Take your time with this, shaping and placing each piece carefully to keep the edges of the numbers crisp and even.

12 Finally, fill in the background with broken yellow tiles nipped to fit between and around the numbers. Remember to keep the spaces between pieces consistent.

13 Now you can tile the edges. Using a ruler and glasscutter, cut the yellow mirror into $3/4$-inch (1.9 cm) strips to match the width of the wood. Snap off the strips with running pliers, then use mosaic glass cutters to snip each strip into rectangles roughly $1/4$ inch (6mm) wide; don't bother measuring, just eyeballing it is good enough. Make these cuts straight, not at an angle. Glue the pieces around the front board's edge.

14 Using the same techniques as in step 13, cut and snip $3/4$-inch (1.9 cm) strips of silver mirror into $1/2$-inch (1.3 cm) pieces, and glue them around the edges of the starburst back board. Leave approximately $1/4$ inch (6 mm) of space where the two sides of a ray meet at the tip. Let the glue dry overnight.

GROUTING

15 Using cleaning tools, carefully remove any glue from the surface of the tile and mirror.

16 Cut and tape a piece of plastic sheeting over the face of the front board, and mask off the board's yellow-mirror edge. Smooth all the tape down securely, so no grout will be able to creep underneath.

17 Mix the blue grout with the phthalo blue pigment and fortifier, and grout the backboard, starting with the mirrored edge. Be careful to fill all the angled joints in the rays, and remember to lift the piece and grout the edge from behind. Then grout the rest of the backboard. Wipe off excess grout with a damp sponge, let the surface haze over, then polish with a soft cloth. Wrap the entire project in plastic and let the blue grout set up overnight before moving on to grout the front board.

18 Carefully remove the tape and plastic covering the front board. Then mask off the black tile along the curve where the rays meet the front board's yellow mirror. Make sure the tape is smoothed down securely. Cover the rest of the back board with plastic sheeting, wrapping the plastic around and under the edges.

19 Mix the white grout with yellow pigment and grout fortifier and grout the front board, again starting with the mirrored edge and finishing with the flat surface. Wipe away excess grout with a damp sponge, let the surface haze over, then polish with a soft cloth. Use cleaning tools to remove any remaining unwanted grout. Wrap the house number in plastic or kraft paper and let cure for three days.

20 Add a metal hanger to the house number's back before hanging.

Sugar-and-Cream Strawberry Planter

Here's a strawberry planter sweetened with decorative sugar bowls, creamers, and

cups amid mosaic flowers. Use dishes from an old matched set, or work out a color

scheme with nonmatching but compatible pieces rescued from a flea market or

thrift store. If you can't find a planter exactly the same size and shape as the one

I used, no problem: Just adapt the instructions to fit your project.

Materials

Ceramic planter, 11 inches
   (27.9 cm) tall, with top opening
   12 inches (30.5 cm) across
10 cups, creamers, and sugar
   bowls (any combination) in
   green and yellow pattern
   (see Note on next page)

4 x 4-inch (10.2 x 10.2 cm)
   ceramic tiles in the following
   quantities and colors:
9 yellow, 9 green, 18 white

Silicone glue
Polymer-fortified thin-set
   tile adhesive
4 pounds (1.8 kg) of white
   sanded grout
Acrylic grout fortifier

Tools and Supplies

Permanent marker
Glass mosaic cutters
Ceramic tile nippers
Old cushion or towel
Masking tape
Pencil
Hammer
Leather gloves
Lazy Susan (optional)
Ceramic tile cutter
Clay modeling tool
Clay cleanup tool
Basic Mosaic Supply Kit (page 22)

Instructions

FIGURE 1

Sample designs for blossoms and leaves

ADDING THE CUPS

Note: A total of only six cups, sugar bowls, and creamers are actually used on the planter in this project. You'll probably need at least 10, however, because not all will break where you want them to when you cut them. Some will split and break in ways that make them unusable. Also, note that throughout these instructions I refer to the cups, creamers, and sugar bowls as cups for simplicity's sake.

1 First, think about where you'll want to place the cups on the planter. Visualize a design with some cups near the top, some near the bottom, and others in between; some spaced near and some away from other cups; some facing right and some left; some with handles intact and some not. If you can't picture them all, decide on the placement of the first two cups; then, after you've cut and glued them in position, you can determine where and how the next should be placed.

2 Hold the first cup up to the planter and determine how much of it you want to remove. You need to leave at least enough for the cup to hold sufficient soil for a plant. With a permanent marker draw a line where the cup is to be cut. Place the wheels of the glass mosaic cutters on the line at the mouth of the cup. Make sure the wheels are facing slightly outward toward the portion of the cup that will be removed. (If your cups are thick

ceramic, you'll need to use tile nippers instead of the glass mosaic cutters.) Once you have the wheels lined up, squeeze the handles. The cup won't break exactly along the mark, but if you're lucky, the portion of the cup you wanted will still be intact. Hold it up to the wall of the planter again. How close is it to actually fitting against the planter? Some space here and there between the cup and the wall of the planter is acceptable—but no more than the thickness of the ceramic tile you'll be placing around the cup. Nibble off any protruding areas, removing little bits at a time, until you get a proper fit. (See the illustration on page 120.)

3 Once you have a cup cut to an acceptable fit, lay the planter down on its side on an old cushion or towel, making sure it won't roll off. Tear off a few foot-long (30.5 cm) pieces of masking tape and have them ready within reach. Squeeze a generous bead of silicone glue around the cut edge of the cup and press the cup in position on the planter's surface. Hold it in place with one hand while you add some additional glue to the joint, both inside and outside the cup. Run a craft stick along the joint to remove any glue globs that could keep the ceramic tile you'll be placing later from fitting close to the cup. Then, while holding the cup in place, secure it with tape.

Jan Hinson, Blue Wave Bench, 1998, 56 x 24 inches (142 x 61 cm), lightweight ferro-cement forms, reset broken tile. Photo by artist.

Run lengths of masking tape from the planter wall, over the cup, and back down to the planter on the other side. Let the glue dry thoroughly before turning the planter to adhere another cup.

4 Turn the planter to the section where the next cup is to be placed, repeat steps 2 and 3, and so on until you've cut, nibbled, glued, and taped all six cups. Make sure you've created a solid, clean joint at each cup before moving on to the next. Of course, after rotating the planter on its side a couple of times you won't be able to turn it again without hitting one of the glued cups. At this point set the planter upright and use a lot of tape to hold each cup in position. Gravity is your enemy; the cups will sag if not taped securely and globs of glue will ooze downward from the joints. Add extra tape where necessary, and use a craft stick to clean away oozing glue. If running glue leaves a gap in a joint, let the joint dry a bit and then fill the space with more glue. With all cups taped securely, let the glue dry overnight.

TILING

5 With the cups solidly anchored, draw blossom and leaf outlines on the planter, to be filled in with colored ceramic tile. The illustration (figure 1) shows examples of these simple designs. Use a pencil to sketch the outlines where you want them, erasing and correcting if you need to. Add enough designs to tie in the color theme and break up sections that would otherwise be nothing but solid white background. Draw some of the blossoms and leaves so they "run off" onto the top and bottom edges and behind cups, as shown in the photo on page 86. When you've sketched the outlines to your liking, go over the lines with permanent marker.

6 Using a hammer and wearing leather gloves, break up several of the yellow tiles, leaving some intact to be cut later into edge pieces. Now use tile nippers to cut the broken tiles into irregular pieces small enough to lie flat on the planter's curving surface.

7 Mix the thin-set tile adhesive according to the manufacturer's instructions. Using tile nippers to shape the yellow tile pieces as needed, fill in the flower blossom outlines on the planter's surface. Take care to nip pieces to match each blossom's edge contours, and fill the middles with irregular shards. Use a craft stick to butter each piece with adhesive; then press it into position. Work from the bottom up so that the pieces you place on the planter's surface will support the ones you put above them. Use a craft stick to clean away any adhesive that comes up into the spaces between pieces, and wipe off the tiles with a damp cloth as you work. When tiling around a cup, place the pieces flush to the cup, up against it. Also, tile the planter's surface as far inside each cup's opening as you can easily reach.

8 Now break up several green tiles and, using the same techniques, fill in the green leaf shapes. If you'd like the grout lines within a leaf to imitate leaf veins, draw the veins in pencil on the planter first, and then place tiles on either side of the lines, so the lines themselves become grout spaces.

9 With all the flowers and leaves tiled, break several white ceramic tiles. Cut, nip, and glue irregular pieces of white tile to the planter until you've completely filled in the background. Remember to keep the spacing between tiles as uniform as possible.

10 Now it's time to tile the planter's top edge and inside rim. Wherever a leaf or flower blossom runs over the top edge, you'll use the same color (yellow for blossoms, green for leaves) to fill in the design on that section of edge. Measure the width of the planter's top edge and estimate how much of each color tile you'll need. Set the tile cutter to the edge width and cut the tiles into strips. Tile the top edge, using tile nippers to cut the strips into narrow rectangular shapes as needed, and buttering and pressing each piece into position as you go. Then, using irregular shards as you did on the planter's exterior, tile down inside the rim at least 2 inches (5 cm). Wrap the planter in plastic and let the adhesive dry overnight.

GROUTING

11 Put the planter on a lazy Susan if you have one. Use cleaning tools to remove any dried adhesive from the surface.

12 Mix the grout and acrylic fortifier. Start grouting the planter on the inside rim, then work grout into the edge pieces along the top. Use a finger to smooth the joints on both sides of the edge.

13 Now work your way down and around the planter, pressing grout firmly into all the spaces. Take particular care to fill the joints along the inside and outside edges of the cups. Use a clay modeling tool to smooth those narrow joints. Grout the planter's surface inside the cups as far as you can reach, and don't overlook the out-of-sight areas beneath the cups. Finally, grout the lower edge of the planter, carefully maneuvering it to work in the grout from underneath.

14 Wipe the grouted planter with a damp sponge. Allow time for the surface to haze over, then polish it with a soft cloth. Remove any stubborn dried grout with a razor blade or dental tools. Carefully carve smooth any rough areas along the grout lines at the joints with a clay cleanup tool, as shown in the photo above.

15 Wrap the planter in plastic or kraft paper and let it cure for three days.

Snake-in-the-Grass
Flower Bed Border

Light playing on black iridescent glass makes these serpents shimmer with color. Make just one slithering snake to border a small garden bed, or make a second snake to face the first. You could even give your snakes patterns like the real ones in your part of the world, or create patterns from your imagination.

Materials

(for one snake)

6 oval stones, 4 to 6 inches
(10.2 to 15.2 cm) long and 3 to
4 inches (7.6 to 10.2 cm) wide
(see Note)
8 x 8-inch (20.3 x 20.3 cm) piece
of grass-green stained glass
12 x 12-inch (30.5 x 30.5 cm)
sheet of black iridescent stained
glass
Silicone glue
2 $\frac{1}{2}$ pounds (1.1 kg) of black
sanded grout
2 ounces (60 mL) of phthalo blue
liquid pure pigment
2 pounds (910 g) of blue
sanded grout
1 ounce (30 mL) of yellow liquid
pure pigment
Acrylic grout fortifier
1 to 2 ounces (30 to 60 mL)
of acrylic paint, color matched
to stones

Tools and Supplies

Black permanent marker
Pencil
Tile-Making Kit (page 19)
Glass mosaic cutters
Masking tape
Small scissors
Clay cleanup tool
$\frac{1}{4}$-inch-wide (6 mm) flat
paintbrush
Basic Mosaic Supply Kit
(page 22)

Note: Use only five stones to make
a shorter snake, or seven stones
for a longer one (as you can see
from the photo on page 91, I did
both.) In any case choose stones
that have at least one smooth, relatively flat side. Their shapes will
vary, naturally, but try to select
stones of about the same overall
size. Remember too that your
stones will be different shapes and
sizes than those I used, so you may
need somewhat more or less glass,
grout, and adhesive. Also, because
my stones were light in color, I
used a dark, rich-colored glass. If
you choose dark or neutral stones
you may want to use a lighter color
glass for better contrast.

Instructions

1 Wash the stones and let them
dry. Put them in front of you
in a straight or curved row—
however you'll be placing them in
the garden after you've mosaicked
them—and arrange them, moving
them around as needed, until you
find the best fit. You want the
stones to rest as close to one
another as possible.

2 When you have the stones
arranged so they fit together
nicely, write in permanent marker on the bottom of each stone
the number that corresponds to
its order in the row. Without
numbers, you can easily lose track
of their order once you start
picking them up and moving
them around.

3 Now use a pencil to sketch
out a snake design on the
rocks. Start with the head, which
should be roughly 2 inches (5
cm) long and 1 $\frac{1}{2}$ inches (3.8 cm)
wide. Then continue drawing the
rest of the snake's curving body
on the remaining stones, making
sure the lines connect properly
from stone to stone. Begin nar-
rowing the body on the next-to-
last stone, to create a taper for
the tail on the last stone.

4 Next, sketch blades of grass in
places where they'll accentu-
ate the snake's curves and add to
the overall composition of each
stone. Think of each stone as its
own little piece of art. The direction in which the grass blades
point is the direction the viewer's

eye will follow. Avoid large, empty gaps. Try to use the space on each stone in the most interesting way possible.

5 When you're satisfied with your design, go over the lines with permanent marker.

TILING

6 Using a glasscutter and running pliers, score and break the black iridescent glass into tesserae roughly ⅜ inch (9.5 mm) square, following the instructions on page 19. Cut just a quarter of the sheet of glass first, then cut more as you need it after you begin tiling. Do the same with the green stained glass, keeping the two colors separate.

7 Tile the snake's head and body, cutting and nipping the black iridescent pieces with the glass mosaic cutters where necessary to shape them to follow the snake's flowing curves. Try to lay the tiles in the direction of the curves; to do this, some tiles will have to be shaped and some won't.

8 Finish tiling the snake's body on all the stones.

9 The blades of grass are easier to tile than the body because they're relatively straight in comparison. Use the glass mosaic cutters to cut and nip the shapes as needed, and glue them in place to fill the grass blades. After you've finished the blades of grass on all the stones, let the glue dry overnight.

GROUTING

10 Clean any dried glue from the surface of the glass with a razor blade or dental tools. Use a craft stick, however, to remove any residual glue on the stones themselves, to avoid scratching them. Scratches will stay and show, ruining your project's clean look.

11 Now it's time to prepare the snake's body for grouting. To do so, you'll need to use masking tape to create an outer line on each side of the snake that exactly follows the snake's contours, leaving a uniform ³⁄₁₆-inch (5 mm) space between the tape and snake for grout. Because the snake curves, you'll have to cut the tape into small sections with scissors and piece them together to create a line that mimics the snake's shape and leaves an even space. Cut as many small pieces of tape as you need to make smooth curves.

12 Once you've outlined the snake's body with tape, do the same with the blades of grass. Then use tape to cover up the rest of the surface (outside the grout space) on the top and sides of each stone. Covering everything that's not to be grouted makes life easier when you're handling the stone while grouting. Make sure that all the tape is flat and stuck securely, especially along the edges of the body and blades, or the grout will creep up under the tape and ruin the clean lines you're trying to create.

Adriano Gemelli, *Entrance,* **1998,** 8 x 4 feet (2.4 x 1.2 m), laminated stained glass door, mirror-mosaic side panel. Photo by artist.

13 Mix the black grout, phthalo blue pigment, and acrylic fortifier, and grout the snake's body on each stone. Work along the outside edges carefully with your fingertip, applying the grout so that it tapers down from the level of the glass to the masking tape. Use your fingers to smooth this bevel when you first apply the grout. Then, after the grout has had a little time to stiffen up, go back over it with a clay cleanup tool and carve a crisp, even beveled edge. Wipe the grouted glass with a damp sponge, let it haze over, and then polish with a soft cloth. If you have a small amount of grout left over, cover it with plastic wrap and save it in case you need it later for a repair job. Remove any stubborn dried grout from the glass carefully using a razor blade or dental tools.

14 Now you're ready to grout the blades of grass. The black grout and the snake's body are exposed, so you'll have to work carefully to avoid getting green grout on them. Check to see if there are any places where the blades of grass and the snake's body intersect or are so close you know you won't be able to keep green grout off them. If there are, you'll have to let the first grout color set up overnight, then tape off those places.

15 Mix the blue grout, yellow pigment, and acrylic fortifier to make the green grout. Then carefully grout the grass blades. Again, use your fingertips to create a smooth, tapered grout line along the outside edges as you apply it. Then use a clay cleanup tool after the grout has firmed up to carve an even bevel.

16 When you're finished grouting and beveling the edges, cover the stones with plastic and let the grout set for 30 to 45 minutes before following the next step. Again, if you have any green grout left over, wrap it up in case you need it for repair work.

17 Uncover the stones and carefully remove the masking tape. If you dislodge any grout in the process, smooth that part of the tape back down or replace it with new tape and fill the gap with leftover grout. Once you've removed the tape from a stone, take a close look to see if you can spot any places where grout crept up under the masking tape and left a less than sharp grout line. If this has happened, carefully rub away as much of the stray grout as possible with a craft stick. Sometimes stains from the grout colorant, rather than chunks of grout, find their way under the tape. To cover these stains and create a crisp-looking grout line, paint over them with acrylic paint mixed to match the color of the stone. Give the paint a few minutes to dry, then wrap the stones in plastic or kraft paper and let them cure for three days.

Jill MacKay and Craigie, *Sculptural Bench,* ***1998,*** 3 ½ x 3 ¾ x 21 feet (1 x 1.1 x 6.3 m), steel-reinforced-concrete structure, ceramic tile surface. Photo by Evan Bracken.

Pillar Planter
Under Glass

Bright splashes of color, color, and more color shine beneath shards of clear, double–thickness glass. Here's your chance to be a wildly creative artiste, dabbing paint here and there, even if you've never before picked up a brush. Simply mix and add colors to your heart's content, using lots of pearlescent pigment to give the paint a shimmery, glitzy look.

Materials

10-inch (25.4 cm) length of
6-inch-diameter (15.2 cm)
aluminum ventilation duct pipe
Form-holding woven wire mesh, 12
x 40 inches (30.5 cm x 1 m)
Round-bodied flowerpot approximately 6 ½ inches (16.5 cm) tall;
bottom diameter, 5 inches (12.7
cm); top diameter, 10 inches
(25.4 cm)
Ingredients for two batches of Basic
Fiber Cement (page 25)
Ingredients for slurry (page 25)
Acrylic paint in the following
colors: cobalt teal, cerulean blue,
brilliant blue, chromium oxide
green, vivid lime green, iridescent rich copper, acra gold, deep
magenta, medium cadmium red
White pearlescent powdered
pigment
2 12 x 16-inch (30.5 x 40.6 cm)
sheets of clear double-thickness
glass
Silicone glue
6 pounds (2.8 kg) of black
sanded grout
4 ounces (120 mL) of phthalo
blue liquid pure pigment
Acrylic grout fortifier

Tools and supplies

Scissors
Duct tape
Fiber Cement Supply Kit
(page 25)
Steel rasps
Lazy Susan (optional)
Artist's large, round paintbrush
Plastic cling wrap
Masking tape
Tile-Making Kit (page 19)
Basic Mosaic Supply Kit
(page 22)

Instructions

BUILDING AND SHAPING THE PILLAR

1 To create the pillar, fold the
wire mesh in half, creating a
double thickness measuring 12 x
20 inches (30.5 x 50 cm). Wrap
the mesh tightly around the pipe,
leaving an extra inch (2.5 cm) of
mesh sticking out at each end.
Fold the extra mesh in, down
over the pipe's ends. Secure the
edges of wire mesh on the interior
of the pipe with small pieces of
duct tape.

2 Make one batch of fiber
cement and one batch of
slurry following the directions
on page 25. Now you're ready to
smooth the first layer of fiber
cement onto the pillar. Work
on one section at a time,
remembering to brush on slurry
just before you apply the cement
with your fingers. Press the
cement firmly into the mesh and
onto the surface of the pipe,
keeping the surface as smooth
as possible and creating an even
⅛-inch (3 mm) coating. Also
work fiber cement into the wire
mesh you folded in on both ends
on the pipe's interior. Don't
worry about the pipe's ridges;
you'll level out the surface with
the second layer of cement.

3 When you've completely
covered the pipe and used up
your first batch of fiber cement,
wrap the project in plastic and let
it set overnight.

FIGURE 1

Building up pillar with fiber cement

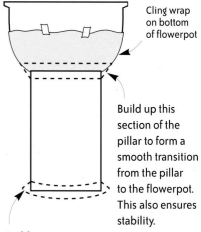

Cling wrap
on bottom
of flowerpot

Build up this
section of the
pillar to form a
smooth transition
from the pillar
to the flowerpot.
This also ensures
stability.

Build out a
graceful flare
at the base
for stability.

4 Mix a second batch of fiber
cement and slurry. This time,
work on building up the areas
along the pipe's ridges, evening
the surface. Also, add fiber
cement around the lower edge so
that it flares out gently, about 1
inch (2.5 cm), giving the pillar a
wider, stable base (figure 1).

5 Next, turn the flowerpot
upside down and cover its base
and the next 3 to 4 inches (7.6 to
10.2 cm) with plastic cling wrap.
Secure the plastic in several places
with bits of masking tape. Turn
the flowerpot right side up and
put it on top of the pillar. Step
back and check to make sure the
pot is resting level on the
pillar; reposition it if it's not.

6 Now, by first slurrying and then pressing on more fiber cement, build up the pillar's upper edge slightly, forming a gentle transition from the pillar to the flowerpot and creating a slightly wider area on which the flowerpot can rest (figure 1).

7 Next, remove the masking tape from the flowerpot and carefully lift the flowerpot straight up off the pillar. The cling wrap should stay behind on the pillar; some will be embedded in the cement. Your job is to extract the wrap from the fresh fiber cement without destroying the built-up edge. Gently pull on a section that you can tell isn't embedded and then gradually ease your way around until you've removed all the cling wrap. If a portion of the new edge breaks off in the process, add a few pinches of fiber cement to rebuild the area. Smooth the edge inside and out after rebuilding any sections.

8 Wrap the pillar in plastic and let it cure for three days. When you unwrap the pillar, use steel rasps to file away any protruding lumps or bumps, smoothing the pillar's surface.

PAINTING

9 While the pillar is curing you can paint the flowerpot— this is the fun part! There's no correct or incorrect method; start with any of the colors. Squeeze about a 1-½-inch (3.8 cm) circle of paint onto a paper plate or palette, and add roughly ½ teaspoon (0.7 g) of pearlescent pigment powder. Then mix in enough water to make the paint slightly thinner than its consistency directly from the tube. Put the flowerpot on a lazy Susan if you have one, then dab the paint here and there on the flowerpot, turning the pot as you work.

10 Now mix another color with pigment and water, and dab it on—and then another color, and another, and so on until you've added all the paint colors and the flowerpot is covered. In the process you'll end up with a widely varied palette of colors, some overlapping, some combining and blending, creating yet more colors. This makes it easy to go back and add a dab of this and a dab of that depending on which colors appeal to you most. Just make sure that the entire flowerpot is covered, including the lip and the top 2 to 3 inside inches (5 to 7.5 cm). Let the paint dry.

11 When the pillar has finished curing, paint it the same way you painted the flowerpot, using the same varied palette and dabbing and blending until the surface is covered with multiple colors. Let it dry.

TILING

12 Tile the flowerpot's rounded lip first. To accommodate the contour and make tiling the lip easier, use narrow rectangles placed end to end in rows. Cut several strips of glass approximately ¼ inch (6 mm) wide with the glasscutter; then nip the strips into lengths roughly ¾ inch (1.9 cm) long. Lay them out in order as you cut them. Now glue a row all around the bottom of the lip. Add another row circling above that, and so on until the entire lip is tiled, including one row around the lip on the inside.

13 Now you have a decision to make: You can add design details—spirals, circles, leaves, or flowers—to your pillar planter as I did (see figure 2 for examples). Or, you can skip the details and simply cover the surface of the pillar and flowerpot with irregular shards. Either way, the combination of double-thickness glass over pearlescent paint is stunning; details just add more interest.

14 If you've decided to add details, cut several ¼-inch-wide (6 mm) strips of double-thickness glass and use glass mosaic cutters to nip them into squares, rectangles, or other shapes needed for the designs you've chosen. If you'll be adding leaf shapes or circles, follow the instructions on pages 45 and 44 respectively. Glue the pieces in place wherever you want to highlight design features.

15 Once you've glued on all the details, or if you've decided not to add any, cut and glue random shapes of glass to cover the flowerpot and pillar's exterior. Use glass mosaic cutters to nip pieces of different sizes and shapes. Spread glue over a small area with a craft stick, then position the pieces. When tiling the pillar's top and the flowerpot's bottom, put the flowerpot atop the pillar first. Then glue the glass pieces in place—but leave approximately 1/16 inch (1.6 mm) of space at the pillar's top edge and another

Marcelo José de Melo, *Blue China Chair,* **1999,** 31 x 22 x 20 inches (78 x 55 x 50 cm), hand-cut china on plywood and wooden chair. Photo by artist.

1/16 inch of space around the flowerpot's bottom edge. This small gap will allow you to put the two finished pieces together without damaging the mosaic.

16 When you've finished tiling both pieces, let the glue dry overnight.

GROUTING

17 Remove the flowerpot from atop the pillar, then clean away any dried glue from the glass on both pieces.

18 Grout the pillar first. Mix half the grout and pigment with fortifier. Then carefully—and I do mean carefully, the glass edges are sharp—press and smooth the grout over the pillar's surface. Remember to grout both the lower and upper edge. Make sure there are no lumps of grout on the upper edge; smooth it nicely, taking care not to fill in the 1/16-inch (1.6 mm) gap you created, so that the flowerpot will sit nicely on the pillar.

FIGURE 2

Sample design elements in clear glass

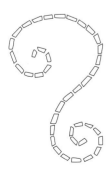
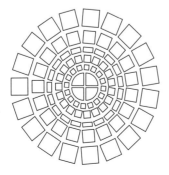

Jill MacKay, *Pebble Mosaic Walkway*, 1998-1999, 17 feet long (5.1 m), constructed in reverse method in molds by section, installed in basketweave, brick walkway. Photo by Evan Bracken.

Jill MacKay, *Tortoise*, 1998-1999, 4 feet diameter (1.2 m), natural pebbles, constructed in reverse method in molds by section. Photo by Evan Bracken.

19 Wipe excess grout off the pillar's surface with a damp sponge, let the glass haze over, then polish with a soft cloth. Use a razor blade or dental tools to clean away any stubborn bits of grout. Wrap the pillar in plastic or kraft paper and cure for three days.

20 Now mix the remaining grout and pigment with fortifier, and grout the flowerpot. Begin at the upper edge, carefully working from inside the lip, up over the top to the lip's lower portion, creating smooth, even grout lines between all the narrow rectangles. Then work your way down and around the body of the flowerpot to the lower edge. Lift the flowerpot (hold it on your lap) and grout the lower edge from underneath. Smooth the grouted edge, again leaving the $^1/_{16}$-inch (1.6 mm) gap intact.

21 Wipe the flowerpot with a damp sponge, let the glass haze over, then polish it with a soft cloth. Clean away any dried grout residue. Wrap the pot in plastic or kraft paper and let cure for three days.

Garden Shrine

Celebrate life's beauty with this ornate shrine, alive with colorful leaf and flower designs and a testament to the rewards of creative endeavor. Follow the pattern's color key to recreate this shrine exactly or devise your own color scheme.

Materials

Cement board, ½ inch
  (1.3 cm) thick
Epoxy putty
Form-holding woven-wire mesh
  (or substitute window screen)
Ingredients for two and one-half
  batches of Basic Fiber Cement
  (page 25)
Ingredients for two batches of
  slurry (page 25)

Vitreous glass tiles, ¾-inch
  (1.9 cm) square in the following
  quantities and colors:
8 to 10 of metallic turquoise
10 to 12 each of beige, brick red
14 to 16 of deep red
22 to 24 each of light blue green,
  metallic light purple
26 to 28 of orange
½ pound (227 g) or 70 to 80 each
  of olive green, light grass-green,
  light baby blue, medium teal
1 pound (454 g) or 140 to 160 of
  metallic deep brown
1 ½ pounds (681 g) or 210 to 240
  of metallic medium pink
4 pounds (1.8 kg) or 560 to 640
  metallic grass-green

12 x 12-inch piece of silver mirror
6 ½-inch (1.3 cm) tulip-shaped
  multicolored glass jewels
Silicone glue
5 pounds (2.3 kg) of blue
  sanded grout
2 ½ ounces (75 mL) of yellow
  liquid pure pigment
Acrylic grout fortifier

Tools and Supplies

Patterns for Garden Shrine
  (pages 146 to 147)
Pattern Transfer Kit (page 42)
Spiral saw with ceramic tile drill
  bit, or heavy-duty utility knife
Clay modeling tool
Potter's rib or 3 x 4-inch
  (7.6 x 10.2 cm) rectangle cut
  from plastic milk jug
Glass mosaic cutters
Lazy Susan (optional, but highly
  recommended)
Basic Mosaic Supply Kit
  (page 22)

Instructions

BUILDING THE SHRINE

1 Using the spiral saw or utility knife, cut a 18 x 24-inch (45.7 x 61 cm) piece of cement board.

2 Using the patterns on pages 146 and 147, transfer the outlines—just the outer lines—for the shrine backboard and shelf onto the cement board. Then cut out the shapes for both sections, again using either a spiral saw or utility knife.

3 Now you're ready to bond the sections together with epoxy putty. Pinch off two pieces of epoxy roughly 1 1/4 inches (3.2 cm) long and knead them together until the putty is uniform in color. Roll out a snake of putty the length of the shelf and about 3/8 inch (9.5 mm) thick. Press the line of putty onto the shelf's surface along the length of the back. Then firmly press the bottom edge of the backboard into the bead of epoxy, making sure to align the sides flush with the shelf's side edges. Use your fingers and the clay tool to push the putty firmly into the full length of the joint. Carefully tip the backboard flat on its back, with the shelf board sticking up, and place a brick or two up against the bottom of the shelf to hold it in place while the epoxy hardens for 15 minutes. If the joint seems weak, press more epoxy on both sides of the joint, wherever it needs strengthening (see photo on page 27).

4 Using a pencil and tracing paper, trace around the arch armature outline, indicated by a dotted line on the pattern. Cut out the arch shape by cutting along the dotted line. Then center the arched-shape piece of tracing paper at the bottom of the backboard. Trace around it with pencil, then go over the line with permanent marker.

5 Cut a 7 x 20-inch (17.8 x 50.8 cm) piece of wire mesh or window screen. Fold this in half lengthwise, creating a double thickness measuring 3 1/2 x 20 inches (8.9 x 50.8 cm).

6 Mix one batch of slurry and a batch of fiber cement. Lay out the folded wire mesh flat on a covered work surface, brush it with a coat of slurry, and then smooth and press fiber cement into both sides of the screen. Don't give it a thick coat; press on just enough to cover the screen, and then smooth both sides nicely. Now bend the cemented screen into an arch shape that matches the arch line on the backboard. With the screen in that position, put a brick on each side to hold the sides in place. You may also need to put a rock or piece of wood on the inside of the arch to keep the walls from sagging inward. Cover the arch with plastic and let the cement set overnight.

7 With the cemented mesh hardened, you can epoxy the arch to the backboard. Knead two 1/2-inch (1.3 cm) pieces of epoxy putty together until the material is a uniform color. Position the arch along the outline on the backboard, then press and smooth a line of epoxy along the inside joints, where the arch meets the backboard and shelf. Let it harden for 15 minutes. Then knead and press more epoxy putty along the arch's bottom outside edges, bonding the arch to the shelf. Use a clay modeling tool to smooth the epoxy. Let it harden 15 minutes.

8 Next, you'll build up the thickness of the arch walls and then create a vaulted interior ceiling. Mix one batch of fiber cement and a batch of slurry. With the shrine laying flat on its back, brush slurry over the joints along the inside of the arch where it meets the backboard and shelf. Then press a layer of fiber cement along these areas, smoothing the joints. Now do the same along the outside joints.

9 Now you're ready to add a layer of fiber cement to the entire arch. Remembering always to slurry the surface first, work your way from the backboard outward, covering the arch inside and out until you've created a total thickness (including the fiber cement on both sides of the mesh) of approximately 5/8 inch (1.6 cm). Use your fingers and a potter's rib to smooth the surface. Pay particular attention to the arch's front edge, which should be level and a consistent 5/8 inch wide all around the opening. When you run out of the first batch of fiber cement, make another.

10 Once the walls are built up you can work on the vaulted ceiling. Simply add fiber cement to the arch's interior so that the ceiling and walls slant inward, becoming much thicker toward the back, creating a vaulted look (photos above). Bring the fiber cement down onto the top and sides of the back wall until the bare, unce-mented arch shape at the back is about 5 inches (12.7 cm) high and 4 inches (10.2 cm) wide. Smooth the fiber cement along the sides and sloping ceiling. When you look into the arch you should be able to see the entire ceiling, because of the vaulting.

11 Finish the base by smooth-ing fiber cement onto all the rough outside edges of the backboard and shelf. Press fiber cement along all the joints, too, to smooth and reinforce them. Wrap the shrine in plastic and let the cement cure for three to five days.

TILING

12 Trace the pattern for the backboard design and transfer it to the cement board using graphite paper. To do this, you'll need to cut the arch shape out from the taped-together trac-ing and graphite papers (see page 41), then position the cut pattern over the arch and onto the backboard. Next, trace and transfer the design patterns for the shelf and outer arch. Go over all the graphite lines with permanent marker.

13 With the shrine on its back begin cutting and gluing metallic grass-green tiles around the backboard's outer perimeter. Cut, nip and shape the glass tiles as needed using glass mosaic cutters. To speed things up, cut several pieces to width first, then glue them in place. Make sure the tiles don't extend over an edge; they should be flush. With the outer perimeter tiled, cut and glue more metallic grass green tiles to fill in the three backboard loops—one over the arch and one on either side.

14 Next, cut and glue olive green tiles in the horizontal areas at the center of the design.

15 Now begins the detail work. This requires care, time, and patience, and can be difficult if you try to hurry—so don't. Stop and take a break when you get tired. Start with the details on the backboard, which should be flat on its back for this. Follow the color chart and fill in the smallest details first, including the six glass jewels, then tile the back-ground areas. On the detail work

make your pieces as uniform in size as possible. For the back-ground, cut varied shapes and sizes. This creates more contrast, which makes the finished piece more interesting. Remember to cut and place your pieces so they follow the flow of the pattern. Use a craft stick to spread glue one small area at a time. Use tweezers to place pieces too tiny to handle with fingers.

16 When you've completed the backboard you can start work on the arch. With the shrine still on its back, cut and glue metallic grass-green tiles on the arch's front edge. Work up from the bottom on each side, then fill in the top. You'll have to cut some pieces at an angle to tile the curve. Mostly, though, you can use full-length pieces cut down in width to match the width of the arch's edge. Let the glue for these tiles dry at least 30 minutes before moving on to the next step.

17 Set the shrine upright to work on the rest of the arch's exterior. Start by filling in the details of the flower on top of the arch and the leaf designs on each side. To fill in the color strips on the sides, use full-length tiles cut to a width of about 1/2 inch (1.3 cm).

18 Next, tile the leaf designs on the shelf and fill in the background. Then tile the shelf's front and side edges with metallic grass-green. Cut each tile just once to width, to match the shelf's width, and glue it with the finished side (instead of the opposite cut side) facing up, to create a more uniform, smoother edge. Let the glue for these tiles dry.

19 Now you're ready to line the inside of the arch with silver mirror. Using glass mosaic cutters, cut the silver mirror into irregular shards, nip them to shape as needed, and glue them in place, tiling the entire inner arch, floor to ceiling.

20 Cut approximately 50 metallic grass-green tiles down to the same width as the edge of the backboard. Beginning on one side at the bottom edge, work your way up the side to the top, keeping the spacing between tiles uniform. You'll need to cut the tiles into smaller lengths at the point where the straight edge curves inward toward the top, in order to keep the pieces laying flat and smooth. Make sure no tiles slip out of position. Tile the edge on the other side the same way.

21 Finally you've come to an easy part. You can tile the back side of the backboard almost entirely with whole tiles. Glue clover green tiles in rows onto the back, starting at the bottom and working upward. Chances are, at least on the bottom rows, you'll need to cut only one tile to fill out the space properly. Put this one cut tile in a different place on each row so it won't be noticeable. Of course, when you get toward the back's top, you'll have to nip and shape the pieces to keep them flush to the curving edge. With all the tiling complete, let the glue dry overnight.

GROUTING

22 Grouting the shrine is a big job that will take an entire day; start early, and allow no interruptions. First, clean any excess dried glue from the surface of the tiles and mirror.

23 Grout the arch and the shelf first. Using ³⁄₄-inch (1.9 cm) masking tape, mask off around the outside of the arch, positioning the tape approximately ¹⁄₂ inch (1.3 cm) out from where the arch meets the backboard. Then run a second piece of tape outside the first, overlapping it slightly, making the taped area twice as wide. This will help keep the backboard clean but allow the grout to fill the joint.

24 Now use the same technique to mask off the backboard where it meets the shelf on each side of the arch, again leaving a ¹⁄₂-inch (1.3 cm) space between the joint and the edge of the tape and again adding a second piece of tape slightly overlapping the first for better coverage. The tape should extend over the outside edge on each side, too.

25 Mix 3 pounds (1.4 kg) of grout with 1 ¹⁄₂ ounces (45 mL) of pigment and enough acrylic grout fortifier to achieve the desired consistency. Grout the inside of the arch first, using gloved fingers to carefully push the material into all crevices and joints. Then grout the front edge of the arch and the edges of the shelf. Position the shrine past the edge of your work surface in order to get grout up under its front and side edges. Smooth the edge grout lines nicely. Then grout the shelf itself and the arch's outer surface.

26 Now it's time to clean the area you've grouted, before the material hardens too much. Cover the grout container with plastic so the unused grout won't dry out. Using a damp sponge, wipe off excess grout from the arch, shelf, and edges. Let the surface haze over, then polish it with a soft cloth and use cleaning tools to remove any dried grout residue. Remove all masking tape and clean away any grout that may have gotten up under the tape.

27 Put the shrine on its back and grout the front surface of the backboard, taking care not to miss any spots. Wipe away excess grout using a damp sponge. Let the glass haze over, then polish it with a soft cloth and meticulously clean away any bits of dried grout using a razor blade and dental tools. This is a big job so take your time, making sure to remove all the residue.

28 Mix the remaining 2 pounds (910 g) of grout with 1 ounce (30 mL) of pigment and enough acrylic fortifier to produce the desired consistency. Set the shrine upright again and grout the edges of the backboard, starting at the bottom on one side and working to the top, then repeating the process on the other side. Then grout the back side of the backboard. Again, wipe away excess grout with a damp sponge, polish the surface with a soft cloth, and use cleaning tools to remove dried grout residue.

29 Wrap the grouted shrine in plastic or kraft paper and let it cure for three days.

Craigie, *Waterfall,* **2001,** 3 x 4 feet (.9 x 1.2 m), glass on glass. Photo by Evan Bracken.

Bold Beautiful Beetle

Here's a garden beetle that never nibbles plants or flowers. Instead, it just sits around and looks good with the sun dancing on its opalescent back. There's no reason for the insect to be lonely, either, because once you've made a mold it's easy to cast as many beetles as you want.

Materials

3 to 5 pounds (1.4 to 2.3 kg)
   of natural clay
6 x 9-inch (15.2 x 22.9 cm) plastic
   food storage container
6 pounds (2.8 kg) of plaster of Paris
Materials for one-half batch of
   Basic Fiber Cement (page 25)

Stained glass:
3 x 6-inch (7.6 x 15.2 cm) piece of
   black opalescent stained glass
3 x 6-inch (7.6 x 15.2 cm) piece of
   light blue opalescent stained glass
5 x 6-inch (12.7 x 15.2 cm) piece of
   ruby opalescent stained glass

3 x 3-inch (7.6 x 7.6 cm) piece of
   blue mirror
Silicone glue
2 pounds (910 g) of black
   sanded grout
Acrylic grout fortifier
10 inches (25.4 cm) of 20 gauge
   (.75 mm) flexible wire
Wire coat hangers
Epoxy glue in syringe
Red, black, gold, and light blue
   enamel paint or fingernail polish

Tools and Supplies

Clay modeling tool
Pencil
Round toothpick
Spray cooking oil
Scissors
Tile-Making Kit (page 19)
Glass mosaic cutters
Basic Mosaic Supply Kit (page 22)
Wire cutters
Needle-nose pliers
Polystyrene foam cup
Small acrylic paint brush

Instructions

1 Using figure 1 on page 108 and the photos and description on page 40 as guides, sculpt a simple clay beetle 6 inches (15.2 cm) long, about 3 3/4 inches (9.5 cm) wide, and 1 3/4 inches (4.4 cm) tall at its highest point (along the middle of the back). Use a clay modeling tool to help you shape the contours, but don't try for a lot of detail; just a basic insect form will do. Remember to slope the beetle outward along its bottom edge to create draft and avoid undercut (see page 40).

2 Spray the inside of the plastic food container with cooking oil and put the clay beetle in it, top side up. Mix the plaster of Paris according to the manufacturer's directions and pour it into the plastic container, filling it to a depth of 1 inch (2.5 cm) above the beetle. Tap and shake the container gently to get rid of trapped air bubbles. Let the plaster set up overnight.

3 Cut away and discard the container. Then remove the beetle from the mold. If it's stuck, pry it out gently with a pencil or other tool, taking care not to scar the plaster. Wipe out any clay sticking to the walls of the mold.

4 Mix half a batch of fiber cement. Spray cooking oil into the plaster mold, coating the inside thoroughly. The oil will act as a release agent, allowing you to remove the cast beetle.

5 Press fiber cement firmly into the mold, pushing out trapped air, which can keep the cement

from taking on the mold's shape. Wrap the filled mold in plastic and leave it overnight.

6 Remove the cement beetle from the mold. If you have trouble getting it out, stick a pencil or dental tool part way into the center of the beetle and pry the insect loose. If this leaves the bottom of the beetle somewhat marred, just press and smooth any loose pieces back down.

7 With the beetle separated from the mold, use the toothpick to carefully make two holes 1/8 inch deep (3 mm) for the antennae, one behind each eye, as shown in figure 1. If the cement has hardened too much for the toothpick to penetrate, use thin wire no thicker than a toothpick. Now turn the beetle over and make holes for the six legs. Make these holes slightly wider and about 5/16 inch (8 mm) deep.

8 Wrap the beetle in plastic and let the cement cure for two to four days.

TILING

9 Following the instructions on page 19, cut the three colors of opalescent stained glass into strips approximately 1/4 inch (6 mm) wide. Then, keeping the colors separate, snip the strips into squarish tesserae.

10 Following the color key in figure 1, glue the tesserae in place, using tweezers if necessary to hold the tiny tiles. Position the tiles in lengthwise rows along the wing sections and center of the back. Place the neck and head

FIGURE 1

Beetle pattern

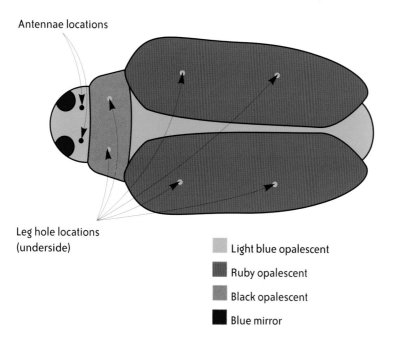

Antennae locations

Leg hole locations (underside)

Light blue opalescent

Ruby opalescent

Black opalescent

Blue mirror

---

wire. Stick the uncurled ends of both antenna wires into the upturned end of a polystyrene foam cup, to hold them in place, and paint the wires with red enamel or nail polish. Allow to dry.

14 Using the wire cutters, snip six 5-¹⁄₂-inch (14 cm) lengths of wire from coat hangers. Bend the six legs into the shape shown in figure 2. Rest the beetle on its back on a towel or cloth and squeeze epoxy glue into each of the leg holes. Then put the legs into the holes. Leave the beetle with its feet in the air until the epoxy has hardened completely. The beetle is now at its most vulnerable; feel free to scratch its belly.

15 Turn the beetle upright and use epoxy glue to attach the two antennae. Wipe away any epoxy that overflows onto the glass. Again let the epoxy set before handling. Paint bands of red, gold, blue, and black enamel down each leg.

FIGURE 2

Leg wire bending pattern

End that attaches to body

---

tiles widthwise. Be careful not to tile over the two antenna holes.

11 Cut two ¹⁄₂-inch (1.3 x 1.3 cm) squares from the blue mirror and nip these squares into circles (see page 44). Nip the circles in half and then in half again. Glue the quarter-circle eye pieces in place. Let the beetle dry overnight.

GROUTING

12 Clean away any dried glue from the surface of the stained glass and mirror. Mix the grout with the fortifier. Then grout the beetle, taking care to work the material into all the spaces between the tiles. Make sure you turn the beetle over and grout the bottom edge from underneath.

Wipe the surface with a damp sponge, let it haze over, and polish with a soft cloth. Use a toothpick to clean out any grout that may have filled the two antenna holes. Wrap the beetle in plastic or kraft paper and let cure for three days.

LEGS AND ANTENNAE

13 Cut the 20-gauge (.75 mm) wire in half, creating two 5-inch (12.7 cm) antenna wires. Using needle-nose pliers, grasp a wire ¹⁄₈ inch (3 mm) from one end and curl it into a tight loop. Then move the pliers up the wire ¹⁄₈ inch and curl the end inward again. Continue moving up and curling the wire by making many small bends every ¹⁄₈ inch, until the first 1 ¹⁄₂ inches (3.8 cm) is spiraled. Repeat this on the second antenna

Spiraling Pebbles Plant Surround

Pebble mosaics have graced artful gardens since the days of the ancient Greeks. This contemporary plant surround presents a new twist: placing the colorful pebbles in a unified direction makes the spirals spin.

Materials

Materials for plant surround base
(page 29)
3 pounds (1.4 kg) of mixed dark
(black-brown-grey) pebbles
2 pounds (910 g) of light
turquoise pebbles
Silicone glue
Polyurethane spray
1-¹⁄₂ pounds (681 g) of dark gray
sanded grout
Acrylic grout fortifier

Tools and Supplies

Tools for plant surround base
(page 29)
Pattern for Spiraling Pebbles Plant
Surround (page 148)
Pattern Transfer Kit (page 42)
Basic Mosaic Supply Kit
(page 22)

Instructions

BASE CONSTRUCTION

1 Make the plant surround base following the instructions on pages 29 through 31.

APPLYING THE PEBBLES

2 Trace one of the spirals from the pattern and transfer it to the surface of the cement cone (see page 41). Position the spiral's open end ½ inch (1.3 cm) up from the cone's bottom edge. Then transfer three more spirals onto the cone, also ½ inch up from the bottom edge and leaving 2 ³⁄₈ inches (6 cm) of space between them, as indicated on the pattern. Go over the graphite lines in permanent marker so they can't be smudged off.

3 Spread out all the dark pebbles and sort them by size and appearance, putting the nicest, flattest, most uniform large, medium, and small pebbles on separate plates. Do the same with the turquoise pebbles.

4 Using a craft stick, spread glue on about a third of one spiral, starting at its innermost, or closed, end. Then begin positioning the turquoise pebbles. Remember that the direction in which you place each pebble influences the spiral's directional flow. Orient narrow or oblong pebbles lengthwise, in the direction of the spiral, rather than across.

5 Finish tiling the spiral, working one third at a time. Then place a double row of turquoise pebbles along the lower border until you get to the next spiral. Glue and tile that spiral one third at a time, continue along the border to the next spiral, and so on until you've completed all the spirals and the entire border.

6 Next, use the dark pebbles to fill in the background space between and around the spirals. Don't worry about the direction in which you place the dark pebbles; their random positions will add contrast, emphasizing the spirals' flow. Do make sure, however, to keep the uppermost pebbles flush with the top edge.

7 Glue a band of the tiniest, roundest turquoise pebbles around the top inside edge to give the surround a finished look. Let dry overnight.

GROUTING

8 Outdoors or in a well-ventilated area, lightly spray the pebbles with polyurethane. Use just enough to coat them, so the grout won't permanently adhere to the pebbles, but not enough to make them look glossy. Much of the beauty of pebbles is their natural, tactile quality. Let the polyurethane dry completely.

9 Mix the grout and fortifier to the desired consistency in one container and fill another with water for cleaning. Apply the grout, making sure to push grout up under the pebbles at the bottom edge and down over the pebbles on the top inner edge. Wipe the entire surface with a damp sponge, let it dry for 10 to 15 minutes until it hazes over, and then polish the pebbles with a soft cloth. Wrap the surround in plastic or kraft paper and let cure for three days.

Starburst Garden Appliqué

A varied glass palette, glinting jewels, a touch of blue mirror—and a star is born. Here are instructions for making the appliqué in the upper right of the photo. The other appliqué is one example of endless possibilties.

Materials

Materials and Supplies for Indirect Mosaic On Mesh (page 54)

Flat-backed glass jewels:
4 5/8-inch (1.6 cm) oval, blue with silver flecks
8 1/2-inch (1.3 cm) tulip-shaped, multicolored
8 1/2-inch (1.3 cm) teardrops, opal with metallic background
9 3/4-inch (1.9 cm) rectangular, opal with metallic background

Vitreous glass tiles, 3/4-inch (1.9 cm) square in the following quantities and colors:
6 to 8 of light grass green
8 to 10 of metallic grass-green
16 to 18 of medium teal
18 to 20 each of orange, cobalt blue, bright turquoise blue

2 x 2-inch (5 x 5 cm) piece of royal blue mirror
2 1/2 pounds (1.1 kg) of black sanded grout
3/4 ounce (22.5 mL) of phthalo blue liquid pure pigment
Acrylic grout fortifier

Tools and Supplies

Pattern for Starburst Garden
   Appliqué (page 149)
Basic Mosaic Supply Kit
   (page 22)

Instructions

1 Following steps 1 through 3 of Indirect Mosaic on Mesh (page 54), transfer the pattern and prepare the appliqué's mesh backing. You should be able to see the design and crosshairs clearly through the mesh. Make sure the mesh's grid is aligned with the vertical and horizontal crosshairs.

2 Start applying materials in the center of the design and, while following the color-keyed template on page 149, work outward. Glue the rectangular opal jewel in the middle first. Then glue two tulip-shaped jewels 1/8 inch (3 mm) apart on each of the middle opal's four main sides, leaving 1/8 inch space all around that center jewel.

3 Using mosaic cutters, cut four triangles 3/8 inch (9.5 mm) long and 1/4 inch (6 mm) wide at the base from medium teal tile. The triangles' tips must be narrow enough to fit between the paired tulip-shaped jewels. Glue them in place, aligning them with the vertical and horizontal crosshairs.

4 Cut four rectangles 1/8 inch (3 mm) wide by 5/16 inch (8 mm) long from cobalt blue tile. Glue the tiny rectangles at the corners of the central jewel, as indicated on the color-keyed template.

5 Now cut four 3/8-inch (9.5 mm) squares from light grass-green tile. Glue these squares in the corner spaces flanking the four sets of tulip-shaped jewels, enclosing the center square.

6 Cut 20 squares approximately 1/4 x 1/4 inch (6 x 6 mm) from orange glass tile. Glue them in place on all four sides of the center square, leaving the corners empty.

7 From the royal blue mirror cut four 3/8-inch (9.5 mm) squares. Glue them in the empty corner spaces flanking the orange squares.

8 Next, glue in the blue oval jewels, aligned with the vertical and horizontal crosshairs.

9 With the central square completed and the inside jewels in place, continue cutting, nipping, and gluing tile pieces for the remaining spaces, using the template as your guide. When cutting

pieces that form or abut the circle's outline, move the mosaic cutter slightly inward or outward, as necessary, to create the curve. Cut square tiles diagonally to form triangles. Cut and nip random shapes to fill in the large and small rays.

10 Finally, glue the rectagular opal jewels at the tips of the small outer triangles, and the teardrop opals at the ends of the rays.

11 Install the mosaic in its permanent location and prepare it for grouting following steps 6 through 10 of Indirect Mosaic on Mesh (pages 54 to 55).

12 Mix the grout, pigment, and acrylic fortifier. Grout, clean, and polish the completed applique following steps 11 through 13 of Indirect Mosaic on Mesh (page 55).

Sparkling Freeform Pinch-Pot Vases

Small, round, tall, tapered, slender, bulging—there are all sorts of possible vase sizes and shapes, so why not make

a variety? Add sparkling glass and mirror set off by brightly colored grout, and you've created a perfect home for

bouquets. Tiling the top edge and inside rim gives theses vases a finished, high-end look.

Materials

(for medium-size vase)

Materials and tools for Making
 Simple Pinch Pots, page 35

Stained glass and mirror
 (see Note):
8 x 8-inch (20.3 x 20.3 cm) piece
 for main background
6 x 6-inch (15.2 x 15.2 cm) piece
 for secondary color
5 x 5-inch (12.7 x 12.7 cm) piece
 for accent color
6 x 6-inch (15.2 x 15.2 cm) piece
 for dark mirror
6 x 6-inch (15.2 x 15.2 cm) piece
 for light mirror

Silicone glue
1 to 2 pounds (454 to 910g) of
 white sanded grout
Liquid pure pigment
Acrylic grout fortifier

Tools and Supplies

Pencil
Permanent marker
Glasscutter
Running pliers
Glass mosaic cutters
Basic Mosaic Supply Kit (page 22)

Instructions

Note: Because these are freeform
vases, the precise designs and colors vary. All the vases, though,
have similar design elements and
a basic color theme that consists
of a main background color, a
secondary color that is a darker
shade of the main color, an
accent color, and light and dark
shades of a mirror color (see the
sample pattern below). The
colors themselves are up to you.
To duplicate the medium-size
blue vase in the photo, follow the
pattern in the illustration, using
glass and mirror colors as indicated and $1/2$ to I ounce (15 to
30 mL) of phthalo blue pigment
to color the grout.

1 Make a pinch-pot vase
 following the instructions
on pages 37 to 38.

2 Using elements from the
 sample pattern below or a
pattern of your own, draw the
desired design on the vase with
the pencil first. When you're
sure you're happy with
the design, go over the lines
with the permanent marker.

3 Choose a color palette of
 stained glass and mirror.
Using the glasscutters, running
pliers, and mosaic cutters as
needed, cut and nip randomly
shaped pieces to fill in the design
elements. Vary the sizes and
shapes of the pieces to create
visual interest. Tile all the details
first (such as the grass blades,
spirals, and small triangles in
my design). Finish by filling in
the background.

FIGURE 1

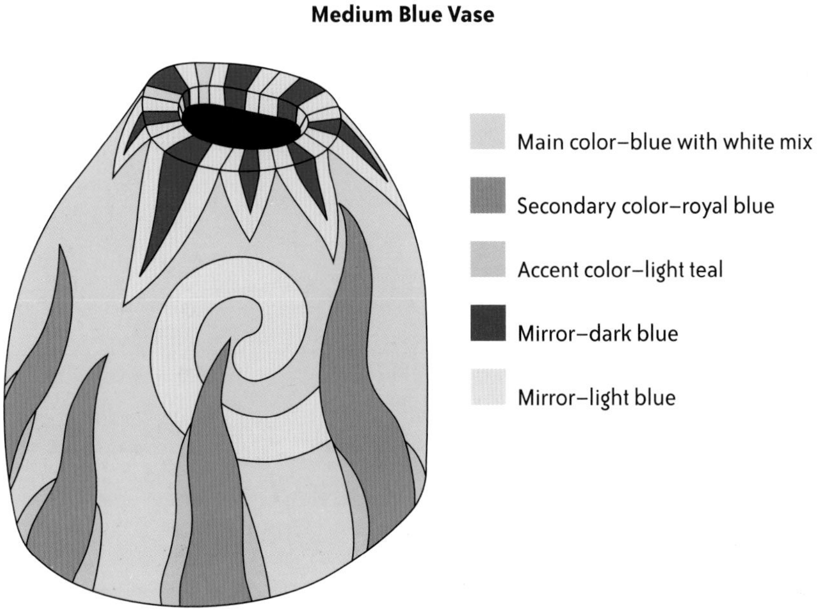

Medium Blue Vase

Main color–blue with white mix

Secondary color–royal blue

Accent color–light teal

Mirror–dark blue

Mirror–light blue

4 When tiling the edge and inside rim, bring the shape and outline of one or more elements (such as the elongated triangle in my design) up and over the lip and down into the inner rim of the vase. Taking the side pattern over the lip and into the interior in this way creates flow (see photo on page 50).

5 Let the adhesive dry overnight.

GROUTING

6 Clean any residual glue from the surface of the glass and mirror with a razor blade or dental tools.

7 Mix and color the grout, adding enough acrylic fortifier to achieve the desired consistancy.

8 Carefully grout the inner rim and upper edge first. Then grout the remainder of the base, moving down and around the body. Be sure to lift and grout the bottom edge from underneath. Wipe with a damp sponge, let haze over, and polish with a soft cloth. Remove any stubborn dried grout with a razor blade or dental tools.

9 Wrap the vase in plastic or kraft paper and let cure for three days.

Craigie, *Untitled*, 1999, 7 x 3 feet (2.1 x .9 m), stained glass bar top.
Photo by Evan Bracken.

Multi-Faceted Gazing Face

Many gardens have gazing balls, but few are graced with a gazing face that seems to know all, see all. Put it in your garden to remind you to open your eyes to all the world's wonders. Though it resembles a gilded treasure from ancient Pompeii, the face is tiled with inexpensive clear glass and homemade gold-leaf tesserae.

Materials

Materials for modeled face
  (page 32)
Metallic gold enamel paint
Acrylic paint in the following
  colors: light cerulean blue,
  dark cerulean blue, cadmium
  red medium, vivid lime green,
  purple, cobalt teal, iridescent
  gold, yellow.
White pearlescent
  powdered pigment
Materials for making gold leaf glass
  (page 14)
2 12 x 12-inch (30.5 x 30.5 cm)
  sheets of double-thickness
  clear glass.
1 5 x 5-inch (12.7 x 12.7 cm)
  piece of silver mirror
Silicone glue
1 1/2 pounds (681 g) of blue
  sanded grout
3/4 ounce (22.5 mL) of yellow
  liquid pure pigment
Acrylic grout fortifier

Tools and Supplies

Tools and supplies for making
  modeled face (page 32)
Pattern for Multi-Faceted Gazing
  Face (page 150)
Pattern Transfer Kit (page 42)
Tile-Making Kit (page 19)
Small pointed paintbrush
Small flat paintbrush
Glass mosaic cutters
Basic Mosaic Supply Kit
  (page 22)

Instructions

1 Make a fiber-cement modeled face following the instructions on pages 32 to 34.

2 Because of the face's contours you won't be able to transfer the entire pattern easily (see page 43). Transfer as much as you can onto the flattest areas using graphite paper. Then draw the rest of the pattern onto the face using pencil. Go over all the lines with permanent marker.

3 Carefully paint the lips, eyelids, eyebrows, and the bridge of the nose with metallic gold enamel, as indicated on the pattern. You'll be tiling these areas with homemade gold-leaf tesserae. The paint will hide any scratches in the gold leaf.

4 Now it's time to paint the rest of the face with acrylic colors, following the key on the pattern. Start with any of the colors. Squeeze about a 1-½-inch (3.8 cm) circle of paint onto a paper plate, add roughly ½ teaspoon (0.7 g) of pearlescent pigment powder, and then mix in enough water to make the paint slightly thinner than its consistency directly from the tube. Use the pointed brush when working in small spaces and the flat brush when painting edges and filling in large areas. Refer to the photo for guidance when combining colors to produce the mixture called for on the pattern, or just trust your own color sense. Let all the paint dry completely.

TILING

5 Follow the instructions on page 14 for making gold-leaf glass. Then, following the instructions on page 19, use a ruler, glasscutter, and running pliers to cut the gold leaf glass into enough ¼-inch (6 mm) squares to tile the eyelids. Spread glue on an eyelid and place the gold-leaf tesserae across the lid in horizontal rows. Repeat with the other eyelid.

6 Now use glass mosaic cutters to nip more gold leaf glass into shards varying in size from small to smaller, some tiny and some larger as needed, and tile the eyebrows, bridge of nose, and lips. Work carefully, maintaining consistent spacing between the pieces.

7 Next, snip the silver mirror into small irregular pieces and glue them in place on the eyes.

8 With the eyes now watching you as you work, use the ruler, glasscutter, and running pliers to make a supply of ¼-inch (6 mm) clear-glass squares and glue them in rows under the eyebrows, along the sides of the nose, and above the lips. Nip and shape the pieces into even tinier squares to cover the nostrils.

9 Tile the rest of the face with irregular pieces of clear glass cut and shaped to follow the direction of the face's design and contours, and to create grout lines that emphasize that flow. Spread glue over a small area at a time, then tile the area, pressing each piece firmly into the glue to eliminate air bubbles that would otherwise show through the clear glass. When you've completed tiling the face, let the glue dry overnight.

GROUTING

10 Clean away any dried glue that's on the surface or filling any grout spaces. Mix the grout, pigment, and acrylic fortifier. With gloved hands, carefully spread and smooth the grout into all the spaces and crevices of the tiled face. Be sure to lift the face and apply grout from the underside to fill the gaps between the glass and the cement along the edge.

11 Wipe away excess grout with a damp sponge. Let the glass haze over, then polish the surface with a soft cloth. Use cleaning tools to remove any remaining grout residue. Wrap the face in plastic or kraft paper and let cure for three days.

Cascading Planter

In this wall planter, "broken" mugs surrounded by colorful glazed ceramic tile provide nooks in which to tuck a plant here, a flower there. I found the small patterned decorative tiles for sale on an Internet auction site, and then bought background tiles in complementary solid colors.

Materials

Cement board, ½ inch
  (1.3 cm) thick
6 tall coffee mugs, 4 yellow and
  2 periwinkle blue (see Note)
25 to 30 decorative tiles in mixed
  sizes and shapes: 1-inch
  (2.5 cm) squares, 1 x 1-½-inch
  (2.5 x 3.8 cm) rectangles,
  1- and 2-inch-diameter
  (2.5 and 5 cm) circles
28 4 x 4-inch (10.2 x 10.2 cm)
  glazed ceramic floor tiles; 7 each
  of the following colors: medium
  yellow, medium pink, maroon,
  and salmon
Silicone glue
Polymer-fortified thin-set
  tile adhesive
3 pounds (1.4 kg) of white
  sanded grout
1 ounce (30 mL) of yellow liquid
  pure pigment
Acrylic grout fortifier

Tools and Supplies

Spiral saw with ceramic tile bit,
  or heavy-duty utility knife
Pencil
Ruler
Permanent marker
Ceramic tile nippers
Ceramic tile cutter
Basic Mosaic Supply Kit (page 22)

Instructions

Note: As you can see from the
photo, only three mugs are used in
this project. I suggest you have at
least six on hand, however, because
not all the mugs will break where
you want them to when you cut them
to fit against the planter board.

CONSTRUCTING THE PLANTER

1 Cut a 10 x 23-inch (25.4 x
  58.4 cm) piece of cement board
using either the spiral saw with a
ceramic tile bit or the utility knife.

2 Using a ruler and pencil,
  measure and draw on the
cement board the background-
color squares and rectangles indicated on the layout on page 151.

3 Visualize how much of each
  of the three mugs you want
showing on the planter board.
Remember that if you want a mug to
house a plant you'll need to leave
enough of it to hold sufficient soil.
If you want the mugs to serve as
small vases for cut flowers you can
leave decidedly less. Consider, too,
whether you want a handle showing
on any of the mugs. I suggest you
leave at least one, for visual interest.
No matter what you decided,
remember that much of this will be

FIGURE 1

Nibbling mug to fit against board

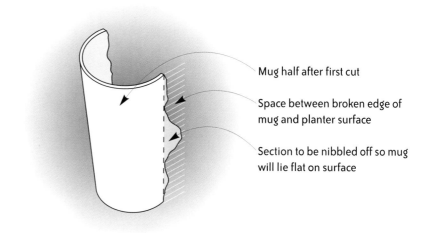

Mug half after first cut

Space between broken edge of
mug and planter surface

Section to be nibbled off so mug
will lie flat on surface

determined by the cutting process
itself. You decide where you want to
make the cut—and then there's how
the break actually occurs.

4 Use permanent marker to draw
  a line on one mug marking the
place for the cut. Align the jaws of
the tile nippers on the mark at the
mug's mouth, with the jaws facing
in the direction of the proposed
cut. Hold your breath, and squeeze
the nippers. The mug will break,
but almost certainly not exactly
along the mark or exactly in half—
but if you're lucky, you'll get something close to it, or at least a useable
portion of mug will be left intact. If
not, try again with another mug.

5 Once you've successfully made
  the first cut on a mug, hold
the mug broken-side down against
the cement board's flat surface.
How close is it to actually fitting
flush against the board? Some
space here and there between the
mug and board is acceptable—but
no more than the thickness of the
ceramic tile you'll be placing

around the mug. Use tile nippers
to nibble off small pieces of the
mug until you get a reasonably
close fit (see figure 1 above).

6 Repeat steps 3 and 4 until
  you have three mugs (one
blue and two yellow) cut and nibbled to an acceptable fit against
the board. Now, using a ruler
and pencil, make a mark that's
2 1/2 inches (6.4 cm) down from
the board's top edge and 2 inches
(5 cm)
in from the left side. You'll be
placing the upper left corner of
one yellow mug here. Squeeze out
a bead of silicone glue along the
cut edge of the mug and align its
upper left corner with the mark.
The mug's top should run parallel
with the cement board's top
edge. Run a craft stick along
the outside joint (where the mug
meets the board) to remove any
creeping glue globs that could
keep the ceramic tile you'll be
placing later from fitting close
to the mug. If you see a gap in
the joint, apply more glue.

7 Now make a mark 10 ½ inches (26.7 cm) down from the top edge of the cement board and 1 ½ inches (3.8 cm) in from the right-hand side. Glue the blue mug there, with its upper right corner on the mark. Finally, glue the second yellow mug in place, with its upper left corner on a mark measured 16 ½ inches (41.9 cm) down from the top edge and 3 ½ inches (8.9 cm) from the left side.

TILING

8 Now determine where among the various background colors on the cement board you want to put the decorative tiles. Play with their placement, moving the different shapes and sizes around until you feel they're evenly and pleasingly arranged. When you're happy with the design, mix the thin-set mortar according to the manufacturer's instructions and mortar the pieces in position. Use a craft stick to butter each tile, then press the tile firmly into place. Scrape off any globs of adhesive that squish out from under the tiles. You don't want dried mortar interfering with the placement of background-color pieces around the decorative tiles.

9 Next, with gloved hands and using a hammer, break up a couple of the yellow tiles. Use tile nippers to cut these broken pieces into smaller shards and shape them to fit around the specialty tile shapes and mugs already in place. Tile in the two yellow areas, buttering each piece and pressing it to the surface. Use a craft stick to clean away any adhesive that comes up into the spaces between the tile shards or onto the surface of the tiles. Use a slightly damp cloth to wipe off the tiles as you work. When tiling around a mug, make sure to place the pieces as close to the mug as possible. Also, tile the board's surface inside the mug as far as you can easily reach.

10 Now, following the pattern and color key, repeat step 9 with the remaining three tile colors, breaking, nipping, and gluing down the tiles in their respective places. Remember to clean off any excess adhesive.

11 Before you start tiling the edge, put something beneath the board—perhaps a few spare tiles—to elevate it and give you access to the edge's underside. Now you're ready to cut the edge pieces. The tile color on the surface determines the color to use on the adjacent edge. In other words, for each section of color on the surface, use the same color tile on that section of edge. Use the tile cutter to cut the tiles into strips as close as possible to ½ inch (1.3 cm) wide, to match the cement board's thickness. As you cut each strip, nip it into short sections and butter and glue the pieces in place. Work your way around the board, changing tile colors as needed to match adjoining sections, until you've finished the entire edge. Make sure the tile pieces don't extend beyond the board's ½-inch width. Let the adhesive dry overnight.

GROUTING

12 Use cleaning tools to scrape away any adhesive from the surface.

13 Mix the grout, pigment and acrylic fortifier and carefully grout the planter. Be sure to fill all the joints around and down inside the mugs as well as the joints along the edges. Remember to grout from the backside on the edge tiles, too, leaving no chunks of grout to dry on the back.

14 Smooth all the grout lines using your fingertips. Wipe away all excess grout with a damp sponge. Let the tiles haze over, then polish with a soft cloth. Remove any stubborn dried grout with a razor blade or dental tools. Wrap the planter in plastic or kraft paper and let it cure for three days.

Night and Day Flowerpot

What's the difference between this fanciful flowerpot with the split-personality face, and the plain storebought version it started out as? You guessed it: night and day. In this project you use a mosaic technique known as "color blending" to fool the eye into seeing a color that isn't really there.

Materials

Ceramic flowerpot, approximately
  10 inches (25.4 cm) tall; top
  diameter 30 inches (76 cm),
  bottom diameter 16 inches
  (40.6 cm)

Vitreous glass tiles, ³/₄-inch
  (1.9 cm) square in the following
  quantities and colors:
  2 to 4 of white
  4 to 6 each of deep red, sky blue
  6 to 8 of light olive
  8 to 10 each of black, light
    grass-green
  10 to 12 each of metallic deep
    pink, bright turquoise blue
  20 to 24 each of metallic deep
    brown, metallic grass-green,
    medium yellow
  ¹/₂ pound (227 g) each of brick
    red, light blue green, light baby
    blue, metallic copper
  1 pound (454 g) each of metallic
    turquoise, metallic baby blue

Silicone glue
4 pounds (1.8 kg) of blue
  sanded grout
2 ounces (60 mL) of yellow liquid
  pure pigment
Acrylic grout fortifier

Tools and Supplies

Pattern for Night and Day
  Flowerpot (page 152)
Pattern Transfer Kit (page 42)
Glass mosaic cutters
Basic Mosaic Supply Kit (page 22)

Instructions

FIGURE 1

TILING THE FACE AND SIDES

1 Transfer the pattern to the surface of the flowerpot. (See page 43.) Go over the graphite lines with permanent marker.

2 Following the color chart on page 152 and referring to the photographs on this page, use the glass mosaic cutters to cut and nip the tiny circles, triangles, and rectangles that make up the eyes, eyelids, and eyelashes. Glue them in place as you cut them, starting in the eyes' middles and working outward.

3 Once you've completed the eyes, cut and tile the nose, then the mouth, and finally the chin. Congratulations; you've finished all the difficult detail!

4 Cut irregular shapes of medium yellow tiles to fill in the crescent moon. Then fill the star on the cheek with metallic baby blue, and the rest of that side of the face with brick red.

5 Now you're ready to work on the metallic copper rays flaring out from the face's "day side." Each ray requires only a few tiles cut to fit: a triangle at the tip, then a series of increasingly wider straight-sided trapezoids. If you're having a hard time seeing the shape that needs to be cut, simply hold the tile up to the spot you're working on and mark the tile where the cuts need to be made. There's nothing wrong with doing this. It may be a little more time-consuming but makes getting accurate cuts easier.

Color Blending

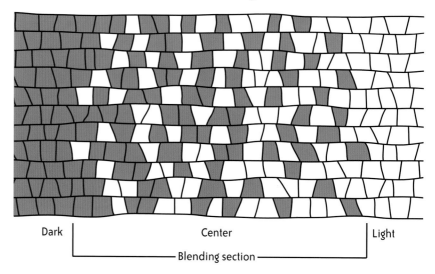

Dark   Center   Light

—— Blending section ——

Gradually intersperse the two tile colors, spacing them evenly so they subtly blend.

6 Next, fill in the areas between and behind the copper rays with metallic grass-green. Then cut and fill the outer row of wide, triangular rays with metallic deep brown.

7 With the flowerpot's face complete, it's time to work on the sides and back. On the front of the pot determine the center-line of the face; bring an imaginary line up from between the eyes, over the top of the flowerpot to the back side. Draw a pencil line extending from there, from top to bottom on the back side, marking the center. Then measure and draw a top-to-bottom vertical line 3½ inches (8.9 cm) away on each side of this center line. Within this 7-inch-wide (17.8 cm) wide section you'll literally blend night (metallic turquoise) and day (metallic baby blue).

8 First, though, follow the color chart and pattern and fill in all the clouds and stars that wrap around the pot. Then tile the backgrounds, working first with metallic turquoise from the center of the chin on the night sky side. Stop when you reach the line that marks the blending section and return to the front of the flower-pot. Again starting at the chin, tile the day sky with metallic baby blue. Stop when you reach the line that starts the blending section.

COLOR BLENDING

9 Now you're ready to blend the areas where the night and day colors come together. Mosaic color blending is the juxtaposition of two colors to simulate a third com-bined color. The gradual blending allows the two colors to move into each other without butting up against each other and creating

contrast. The human eye is tricked into seeing the third or blended color rather than either of the two. As you fill in from the sides of the blending section and work toward the center, intersperse the two colors evenly, combining their placement as shown in the schematic (figure 1). Also, cut the tiles less irregularly and more rectangular to make the blending easier; you want to mix the two colors evenly to achieve a subtle blend.

10 For the next step, you'll need enough brick red tiles to circle the flowerpot's top lip. Using glass mosaic cutters, cut all the tiles in half, but keep the two halves of each tile together on your work surface. Now glue each halved tile in place on the lip, with the center cut running horizontally. Keep the spacing between the halves and between the separate tiles uniform to give the rim a professional look.

11 When you're finished tiling, allow the flowerpot to dry overnight.

GROUTING

12 Clean any dried glue off the surface of the tiles. Mix the grout, pigment, and fortifier.

13 Grout the flowerpot's lip first, making sure to create smooth grout lines along the outside and inside edges.

14 Grout the rest of the flowerpot. Remember to lift the pot and grout the bottom edge at the base. Smooth this edge so that your flowerpot will sit correctly. If you leave any grout chunks under there your flowerpot will wobble.

15 Wipe the grout with a damp sponge, allow the surface to haze over, and polish with a soft cloth. Clean any stubborn spots with a razor blade or dental tools. Wrap the pot in plastic or kraft paper and allow to cure for three days.

Jan Hinson, *Hommage à L.*, 1997,
42 x 28 inches (107 x 71 cm), lightweight ferro-cement forms, reset broken tile.
Photo by John Birchard.

Cheryl's Spirited Tabletop

When my editors asked me to include a small outdoor table in this book, I decided to offer an invitation to friends: Lend me your table and I'll give it a mosaic makeover. Cheryl, the friend whose table I used, is a wonderful artist who loves working with color. Her home is a testament to this—she has a polka-dotted kitchen. So I created a design that reflects her spirit for decorating.

Materials

11 x 20-inch (27.9 x 50.8 cm)
   piece of 1-inch (2.5 cm)
   rot-resistant wood (see Note)
6 x 6-inch (15.2 x 15.2 cm) piece
   of rose mirror
6 x 8-inch (15.2 x 20.3 cm) piece
   of purple mirror
12 x 12-inch (30.5 x 30.5 cm)
   sheet of rust mirror

Stained glass:
2 x 2-inch (5 x 5 cm) piece of rust
2 x 2-inch (5 x 5 cm) piece
   of yellow
4 x 4-inch (10.2 x 10.2 cm) piece
   of teal blue
4 x 4-inch (10.2 x 10.2 cm) piece
   of bright pink with white mix
4 x 4-inch (10.2 x 10.2 cm) piece
   of medium pink with white mix
6 x 6-inch (15.2 x 15.2 cm) piece
   of light blue
6 x 6-inch (15.2 x 15.2 cm) piece
   of blue with white mix
6 x 6-inch (15.2 x 15.2 cm) piece
   of mottled green
6 x 6-inch (15.2 x 15.2 cm) piece
   of purple

Silicone glue
1 ½ pounds (681 g) of white
   sanded grout
1 ounce (30 mL) of purple liquid
   pure pigment
Acrylic grout fortifier

Tools and Supplies

Pattern for Cheryl's Spirited
   Tabletop (page 153)
Pattern Transfer Kit (page 42)
Scroll saw
Sandpaper
Wood sealer
Glass mosaic cutters
Lazy Susan (optional)
Tile-Making Kit (page 19)
Basic Mosaic Supply Kit (page 22)

Instructions

Note: Cheryl's table has a fold-out
metal base on which the tabletop
rests. If you can't find something
similar, just adapt the design to
what you can find. You could
easily change the design to
accommodate a small, round
cafe-style tabletop, for instance.

1 Transfer the pattern onto the
wood (see page 41). Be sure to
go over the graphite lines with
permanent marker.

2 Using a scroll saw, carefully
cut out the tabletop. Sand any
rough edges smooth.

3 Apply two coats of outdoor
wood sealer to the tabletop,
including the edges, allowing
drying time between coats. (You
may have to do just one side and
the edges first, then the other
side.) Let the tabletop dry
completely overnight.

Candace Bahouth, *Fountain*, 1999, 18 x 22
inches (45.7 x 55.8 cm), cement base, broken
china, tessera, mirror. Photo by Debbie Patterson.

TILING

4 Now you're ready to begin
tiling. Start with the three large
spirals. Cut several rows of purple
mirror roughly ³/₈ inch (9.5 mm)
wide. Then, using the glass mosaic
cutters, snip the rows into squares
as you work, gluing the squares
into place within the spirals.

5 Next, fill in the small squiggles
between the spirals. Cut
several ¼-inch-wide (6 mm)
rows of rose mirror, snip them
into squares, and glue them in
position as shown on the pattern.

6 With these design elements
completed, follow the color
chart and fill in the circles and
spaces around them by nipping
and gluing irregular shapes of
stained glass. Notice that on each
of the three sides, at least one of
the polka-dot circles spills over
the side onto the edge. Fill these
edge sections as you go, placing
the pieces in a double row. At
this stage a lazy Susan can be an
especially big help because it allows
you to turn the object without
touching (and possibly knocking
off) freshly glued edge pieces.

7 Now finish the edges with rust mirror. Cut several 1-inch-wide strips of mirror using a glasscutter and running pliers. Then snip the strips into slender rectangles with glass mosaic cutters and glue the pieces in place. You'll have to cut the rectangles especially slim at points where the edge curves sharply inward (see photo above).

8 Let the glued tabletop dry overnight.

GROUTING

9 Before grouting, put the tabletop on something that raises it slightly off the work surface. I used an old book, but anything that will allow you to get your fingers up under the wood to grout the bottom edge will do.

10 Now mix the grout, pigment, and fortifier. Smooth on the grout carefully, making sure to fill all the spaces. Take care, as always, not to cut yourself on the glass, and exercise particular caution when pushing the grout into hard-to-reach areas of the curving edge. I cut myself big time on this piece!

11 Be sure to press the grout firmly into both the top and bottom edge lines, filling the bottom edge from underneath. Smooth the edge lines with a finger.

12 Wipe the grouted surface with a damp sponge. Allow the glass to dry a few minutes and haze over; then polish with a soft cloth. Clean away any remaining dried grout residue. Wrap the tabletop in plastic or kraft paper and cure for three days.

Lily Yeh and James "Big Man" Maxton, Angel Alley (above; detail, left), 1991, 8 x 25 feet (2.4 m x 7.5 m), mixed tile on stucco wall.

Photo by Lily Yeh.

Reflecting Birdbath with View

What bird could resist taking a dip in this elegant birdbath, complete with stream-side scenery and a perch for sunning? For some of the large leaves I used green glass gems to create a dimensional, jewel-like effect. Tiling the wire armature to create the extended branch's foliage and flower petals is challenging but worth the effort; just take your time.

Materials

Tile backerboard (mesh-reinforced cement board) ½ x 24 x 36 inches (1.3 x 70 x 91.5 cm)

Epoxy putty

Ingredients for two batches of Basic Fiber Cement (page 25)

Ingredients for slurry (page 25)

Materials for Wire Branch and Flower (page 35)

Stained Glass:

1 4 x 4-inch (10.2 x 10.2 cm) piece of orange

1 6 x 6-inch (15.2 x 15.2 cm) piece of light blue

1 12 x 12-inch (30.5 x 30.5 cm) sheet of dark blue with ivory mix

2 12 x 12-inch (30.5 x 30.5 cm) sheets of brown

1 12 x 12-inch (30.5 x 30.5 cm) sheet of honey opal white

1 12 x 12-inch (30.5 x 30.5 cm) sheet of light and dark green with ivory mix

2 12 x 12-inch (30.5 x 30.5 cm) sheets of iridized pale blue and white

1 12 x 12-inch (30.5 x 30.5 cm) sheet of teal with white mix

2 12 x 12-inch (30.5 x 30.5 cm) sheets of iridized dark green

17 3 ¼ inch (80 mm) leaf-shaped green glass jewels

1 12 x 12-inch (30.5 x 30.5 cm) sheet of light blue mirror

Silicone glue

6 pounds (2.7 kg) of blue sanded grout

Yellow liquid pure pigment

Acrylic grout fortifier

4 ounces (120 mL) of brown acrylic paint

2 ounces (120 mL) of green acrylic paint

2 ounces (60 mL) of blue acrylic paint

Grout sealant

Tools and Supplies

Pattern for Reflecting Birdbath
    with View (pages 154 to 155)
Pattern Transfer Kit (page 42)
Spiral saw with ceramic tile drill bit
Heavy-duty utility knife
Clay modeling tool
Fiber Cement Supply Kit
    (page 25)
Tools for Wire Branch and Flower
    (page 35)
Tile-Making Kit (page 19)
Glass mosaic cutters
Lazy Susan (optional)
Masking tape
Basic Mosaic Supply Kit
    (page 22)

Instructions

MAKING THE BASIC BIRDBATH STRUCTURE

1 Using the spiral saw or utility knife, cut the backerboard into the five section pieces on the cutting list.

2 Transfer the patterns for the back and base onto section pieces A and B respectively. (See Transferring Patterns, page 41.) Go over the graphite lines with permanent marker. Then cut around the outlines to create the back and base sections.

3 Press a line of kneaded epoxy putty about ³/₈ inch (9.5 mm) thick along the rear outside edge of the base, making sure the putty is sticking well. Then push the back flush up against the puttied edge, vertical and with the back's sides aligned to the base, so the two pieces form a 90° angle. Use your fingers and the clay tool to

press the putty firmly into the entire joint so that it adheres to both boards. Keep the epoxy as smooth as possible. If necessary, knead and press in more putty to completely fill the joint. Then carefully lay the assembly on its back with the base board vertical. Stand bookends or bricks on end, on each side of the base to keep it from moving. Let the epoxy harden for at least 15 minutes.

4 Next, set the piece upright. Hold one of the side strips (section C) atop and along one side of the base. Mark the strip at the point where the base's front corner begins to curve. Draw a vertical line at that mark, then another roughly 1 inch (2.5 cm) from that, and a third 1 inch (2.5 cm) from the second (figure 1). Then, using a utility knife and ruler, score the outside surface of

Cutting List For Backerboard Section Pieces

Code	Description	Qty	Dimensions
A	Back	1	12" x 16" (30 x 40 cm)
B	Base	1	10 ½" x 12" (26.7 x 30 cm)
C	Sides	2	2" x 12" (5 x 30 cm)
D	Front	1	2" x 7 ¾" (5 x 19.7 cm)

FIGURE 1

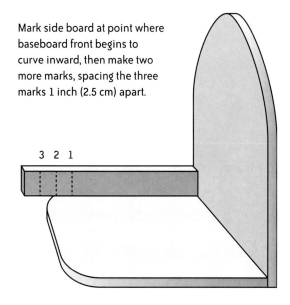

Mark side board at point where baseboard front begins to curve inward, then make two more marks, spacing the three marks 1 inch (2.5 cm) apart.

3 2 1

the cement board along each of the three marks. Align the first score with the edge of a table and gently apply pressure until the piece snaps; it will break but will remain attached to the main piece by the board's mesh. Now snap the other two score lines, producing a side piece with three flexible sections at one end. Repeat these steps with the second side strip.

5 Position one of the side strips on top of the base, with the solid end butted up against the backboard and the flexible, scored section curving around the corner (figure 2). Make a mark on the base's front where the side strip ends. Repeat on the other side.

6 Press a line of kneaded epoxy along one of the base's side edges from the back to the mark you made near the front. Push the side strip onto the putty, making sure the strip is aligned with the base's side and butted up firmly against the back. Support the strip with one hand, keeping it perfectly vertical, while you push the putty into the joint using your fingers and the clay tool. Smooth the epoxy on both sides of the joint. Hold the piece in place until the epoxy hardens enough that the side doesn't lean. Then position and putty the other side strip in place.

7 Trim the front piece (section D) with a utility knife if necessary to make it fit between the two side pieces. Then epoxy the front in place, making sure to fill and smooth the joint front and back. You've now completed the basic birdbath structure.

APPLYING THE FIBER CEMENT

8 Make one batch of fiber cement and one batch of slurry. Now you're ready to apply a smooth layer of fiber cement over all the joints, gaps, and rough edges. Work on one small area at a time, always brushing on slurry just before you apply the cement with your fingers. Start on the inside of the basin. Fill in any gaps in the scored side pieces first, brushing on slurry to keep the surface wet and applying about a half-handful of fiber cement at a time. Fill the spaces as evenly as you can, matching the thickness of the board plus about $1/8$ inch (3 mm). Then press an even, $1/8$-inch layer of fiber cement along all the inside joints, slurrying first and smoothing afterward, forming a gentle transition wherever two pieces meet. Dip your fingers in water and use them to smooth the surface as you go.

9 Next, do the same on the exterior, first filling in the large gaps in the scored side pieces plus about $1/8$ inch (3 mm), then smoothing a $1/8$-inch layer over all the joints, again working one small area at a time and always slurrying first.

FIGURE 2

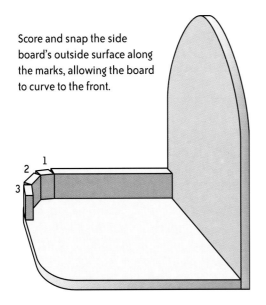

Score and snap the side board's outside surface along the marks, allowing the board to curve to the front.

10 Now apply a layer of cement over all the edges, to smooth them (see page 26). Start at the top and work down the sides, then do the basin edges. Keep the edges as flat and uniform as possible to make applying the mosaic easier. If needed, add cement to the joint on the back side where the backboard and base meet. If you did an especially good job of epoxying them together, there'll be no gaps and you may be able to skip this. In any case, if your epoxy work is bumpy, smooth on enough fiber cement to level the surface.

11 Finally, wrap the base in plastic and let it cure for three days.

ADDING THE WIRE BRANCH AND FLOWER

12 While you're waiting for the base to cure, you can make the birdbath's wire branch and flower. Follow the instructions on pages 35 to 36.

13 With the branch completed and the birdbath fully cured, secure the branch to the left side of the backboard edge, approximately 12 inches (30.5 cm) up from the base. Thoroughly knead together two $1/4$-inch (6 mm) pieces of epoxy. Press the putty around the lower inch or so of the main branch, and bring it down and around the edge surface, creating a smooth transition from wire to board. Add more putty if necessary to create a strong connection. Hold the branch in place until the epoxy hardens.

TILING THE BIRDBATH

14 Use black permanent marker to go over any portions of the backboard and base patterns that were covered up during epoxying and cementing. Then, following the template on page 154, use a glasscutter and glass mosaic cutters, as needed, to cut out the green leaf shapes and white flower petals for the backboard. Cut and nip each petal and leaf into shape and, with the birdbath flat on its back (preferably on a lazy Susan to make maneuvering easier) glue them in place. Cut, nip, and glue the tiny orange flower center pieces, too. Then glue the green glass jewel leaves in position. The jewels add dimension, but, of course, aren't absolutely necessary. If you can't find suitable leaf-shaped jewels, just substitute pieces cut to shape from the same color glass you used for the other leaves.

15 Next, cut and glue tapered sections of brown glass to create the limbs and branches.

16 The background in the design on the backboard mixes several glass colors and types; dark blue, blue mirror, and a random combination of pale blue and teal with white mixes. The design pattern shows where to place the mirror and the darkest shades of blue, but for the rest, you can simply follow your instincts and have fun fitting the colors and shapes together. The effect you're trying to achieve is one of looking through a tree branch out over a river or lake. Thus the direction of the background pattern (behind the branch) should be mainly horizontal. Shape the pieces accordingly, using the flow of colors in the glass and the grout lines between pieces to create the illusion.

17 With the backboard completed, turn the birdbath upright and tile the floor of the basin. Again, cut and shape the primary areas indicated on the template first and then fill in the background, giving it horizontal direction. The floor pattern portrays a rippling, watery reflection of the image on the backboard. When you've finished the floor, cut and place random shapes of blue mirror around the basin's inner sides.

18 Now you're ready to tile the edges with dark brown glass. Using a glasscutter and ruler, cut seven 12-inch (30.5 cm) strips ½ inch (1.3 cm) wide, to equal the cement board's thickness. Then with the mosaic cutters, nip each strip on a slight angle into sections roughly ¾ inch (1.9 cm) wide. Lay out the pieces on your work surface as you cut, keeping them in order.

19 Tile the backboard's edge first. Start on one side at the base and work your way up to the center of the top, spreading glue and placing pieces on a few inches of edge at a time. Then start at the base on the other side and work upward again. At the point where each side curves inward toward the top, you'll have to nip pieces into smaller sizes to maintain a smooth curve. Remember, as always, to keep the spacing between pieces uniform.

20 Next, tile the basin's edge. Start on one side where the basin meets the backboard and work around the edge to the backboard on the other side.

21 Finally, mosaic the entire exterior with dark green iridized glass, cutting and gluing randomly shaped pieces on the front, sides, and back. Nip small pieces for the front's rounded corners, to keep them smooth. You can use relatively large pieces for the flat surfaces, especially the back side. Still, try to create visual interest by mixing and varying the pieces' shapes, sizes, and shades.

TILING THE WIRE LEAVES AND FLOWER

22 Now it's time to tile the wire branch's leaves and flower. Use the same glass colors you used for the backboard's leaves and flowers. Measure one of the epoxy flower petals and, with a glasscutter and glass mosaic cutter, cut and nip a petal shape slightly smaller than the measured petal. Spread a bit of glue on the epoxy petal and position the cut glass. Then measure, cut, and place the remaining petals. Remember to nip and glue a tiny orange circle for the blossom center.

23 Next, measure, cut, nip, and tile each branch leaf. Follow the steps on page 45, Cutting a Simple Leaf Shape, to create the basic leaf sections. Keep each leaf's pieces together, loosely reconstructed in front of you. Because the branch leaves are small and curved, you'll need to nip the diagonal sections into tinier pieces to keep the tiled surface even. Work methodically, one leaf piece at a time, nipping it down and gluing it in place, using tweezers if necessary. Tile each leaf carefully, creating grout lines that resemble leaf veins.

24 Congratulations; you've finished tiling the birdbath. Let all the glue dry for 24 hours. Then use cleaning tools to remove any residual glue on the glass or in the grout lines.

GROUTING

25 Tape a piece of plastic sheeting over the basin, covering all but the joints where the base and sides meet the backboard. Because there's so much surface area, you'll need to grout the birdbath in two sections—the backboard first, then the basin. If you try to grout the entire piece at once you won't be able to clean it all before the grout dries rock hard, which makes for tough going.

26 Mix 3 pounds (1.4 kg) of grout and apply it to the entire backboard. Work on the back and then the front. If you used glass jewels for some of the leaves, be sure you press grout firmly into all the spaces around the gems. Grout the backboard's edges last.

27 Sponge off the backboard, wait until the glass hazes over, then clean away any excess dried grout and polish the surface. (If you used glass jewels, be careful not to dig or wipe away too much grout around them.) If you have enough time to grout and clean the other half of the birdbath, go on to the next step. Otherwise, wrap the piece in plastic and wait till the next day.

28 Uncover the basin and sweep or vacuum out any bits of dried grout that may have fallen into it. Mix the remaining three pounds (1.4 kg) of grout and apply it to the basin. Work on the interior first, then the exterior, then the edges. Also carefully grout the surface and edges of the flower on the extended branch. Sponge, clean, and polish the grouted surfaces.

29 Before you grout the branch leaves, mix a small quantity of the remaining blue grout with a drop of yellow liquid pigment—just enough to produce a suitably green color. Then, while supporting the branch with one hand, press the grout into the grout leaves and around their edges. Carefully sponge, clean, and polish the glass.

30 Paint the epoxied branch brown, the backs of the leaves green, and the undersides of the petals blue. Let the paint dry, then wrap the entire birdbath in plastic and let it cure at least three days. After the grout has thoroughly cured, apply grout sealant to the basin's grouted joints and edges. Allow the sealant to dry for at least a day before you fill the basin with water.

Xuan My Ho, *Four Seasons* **(***The Fall***, chair detail, left), 2001,** table 3 feet (91 cm) diameter, chairs 15 x 15 inches (38.1 x 38.1 cm), china, marbles, ceramic tiles. Photo by artist.

Project Templates

Looking Glass Garden Stake

(page 58)

Silver mirror

Blue-green-yellow mix stained glass

Green mirror

Red-orange mix stained glass

Rose stained glass

Enlarge by 200% and again by 144%

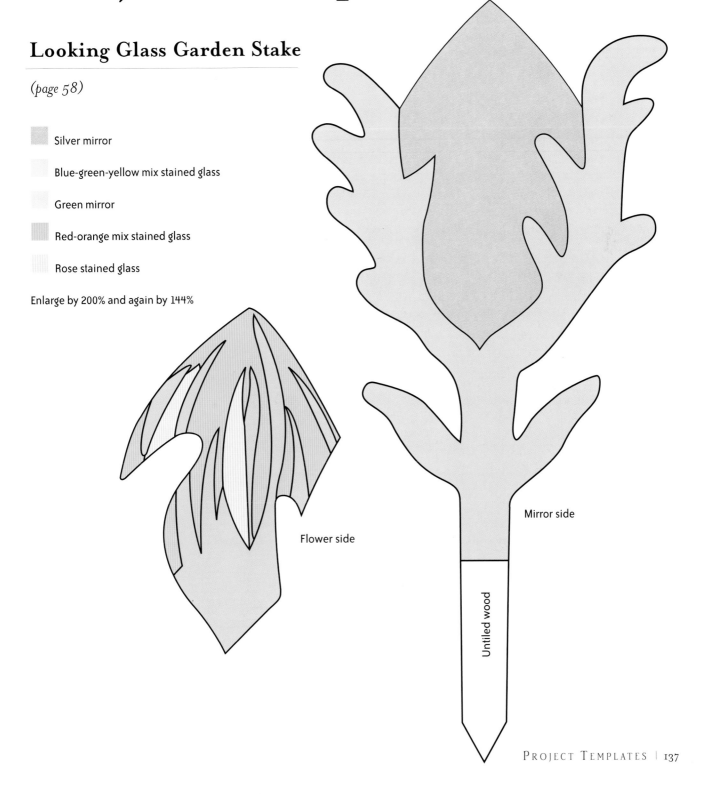

Flower side

Mirror side

Untiled wood

Pebble Mosaic Flowerpot

(page 62)

■ Turquoise pebbles

☐ Dark pebbles (background)

Enlarge by 200%

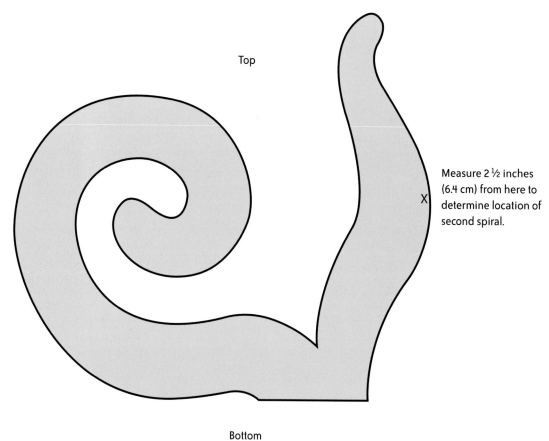

Top

X

Measure 2 ½ inches
(6.4 cm) from here to
determine location of
second spiral.

Bottom

Mosaic Accent Brick

(page 65)

Polished agate slice

Slate blue ceramic triangle

Blue ceramic leaf
S = small
M = medium
L = large

Turquoise/teal pebble

Dark teal ceramic

Combination of blue with white mix
stained glass and light blue mirror

Blue/white ring mottled stained glass

Copy at 100%

Ceramic Tile Plant Surround

(page 69)

Green decorative pattern ceramic tile

Dark green ceramic tile

Light green ceramic tile

Enlarge by 200% and
again by 138%

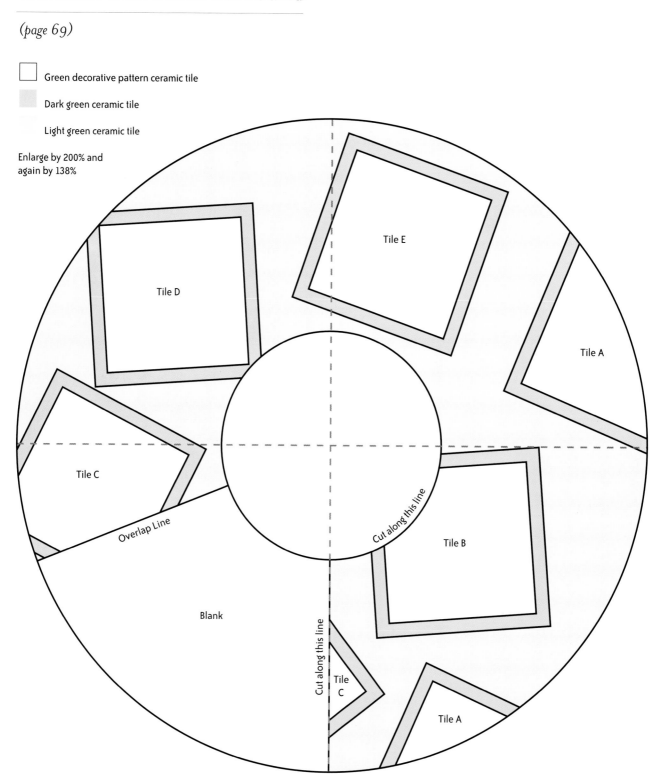

Tile E

Tile D

Tile A

Tile C

Overlap Line

Tile B

Cut along this line

Blank

Cut along this line

Tile C

Tile A

Onion Dome Birdhouse/Left side pattern

(page 74)

 Deep brown

Goldenrod small ceramic leaf

Baby blue ceramic leaf (size on pattern)
S = small
M = medium
L = large

Periwinkle blue small ceramic leaf

Teal blend

Metallic gold

Copy at 100%

Onion Dome Birdhouse/Right side pattern

(page 74)

Deep brown

Olive green small ceramic leaf

Baby blue ceramic leaf (size on pattern)
S = small
M = medium

Periwinkle blue small ceramic leaf
S = small
L = large

Teal blend

Metallic gold

Copy at 100%

Onion Dome Birdhouse/Front pattern

(page 74)

Cutout area/perch hole

Metallic gold

Black

Dark teal

Dark green small ceramic leaf

Light green small ceramic leaf

Gold-leaf glass

Copy at 100%

Not Your Ordinary House Number

(page 83)

☐ Black

☐ Mustard yellow

☐ Royal blue

☐ Red

☐ Orange

☐ Slate blue

☐ Kelly green

Enlarge by 200%
and again by 126%

Back board   Dotted line indicates front board outline.

Not Your Ordinary House Number/Styled numbers

(page 83)

Enlarge as needed

Garden Shrine/Arch and shelf

(page 100)

Metallic grass-green

Olive green

Light grass-green

Deep red

Light baby blue

Metallic deep brown

Metallic light purple

Medium teal

Light blue-green

Orange

Metallic medium pink

Metallic turquoise

Enlarge by 200%
and again by 117%

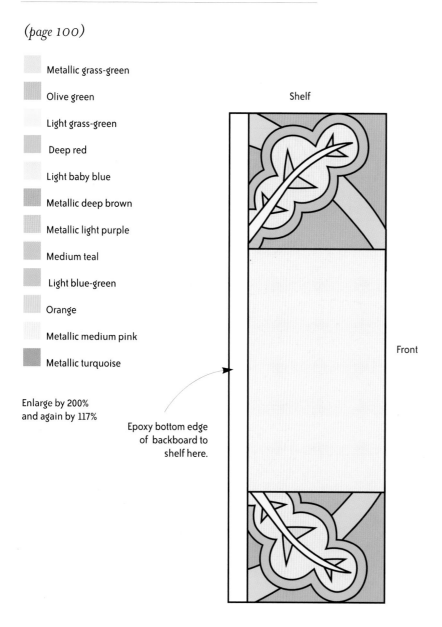

Shelf

Front

Epoxy bottom edge
of backboard to
shelf here.

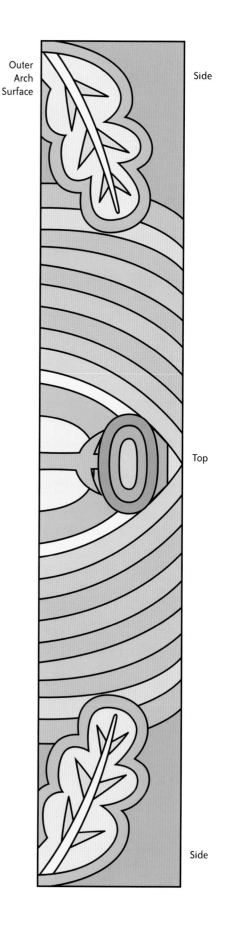

Outer
Arch
Surface

Side

Top

Side

Garden Shrine/Backboard

(page 100)

Metallic grass-green

Olive green

Light grass-green

Brick red

Deep red

Light baby blue

Metallic deep brown

Metallic light purple

Medium teal

Light blue-green

Orange

Metallic medium pink

Silver Mirror

Metallic turquoise

Beige

Glass jewel

Enlarge by 200%
and again by 117%

Arch armature outline—trace on dotted line

Spiraling Pebbles Plant Surround

(page 109)

◼ Light turquoise pebbles

▦ Mixed dark pebbles

Enlarge by 200% and
again by 138%

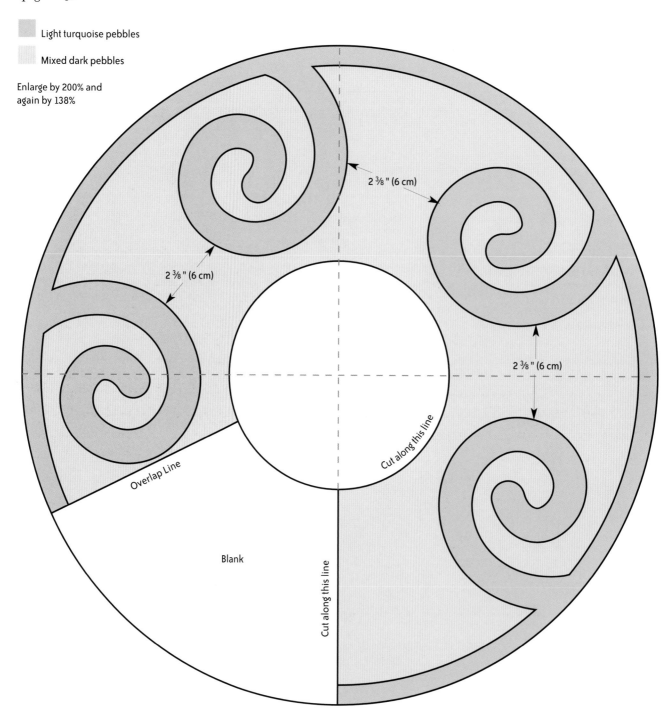

2 ³⁄₈ " (6 cm)

2 ³⁄₈ " (6 cm)

2 ³⁄₈ " (6 cm)

Overlap Line

Cut along this line

Cut along this line

Blank

Starburst Garden Appliqué

(page 111)

Opal rectangular jewel

Multicolor tulip jewel

Orange

Light grass green

Medium teal

Bright turquoise blue

Cobalt blue

Oval jewel

Metallic grass green

Opal teardrop jewel

Royal blue mirror

Enlarge by 175%

Top

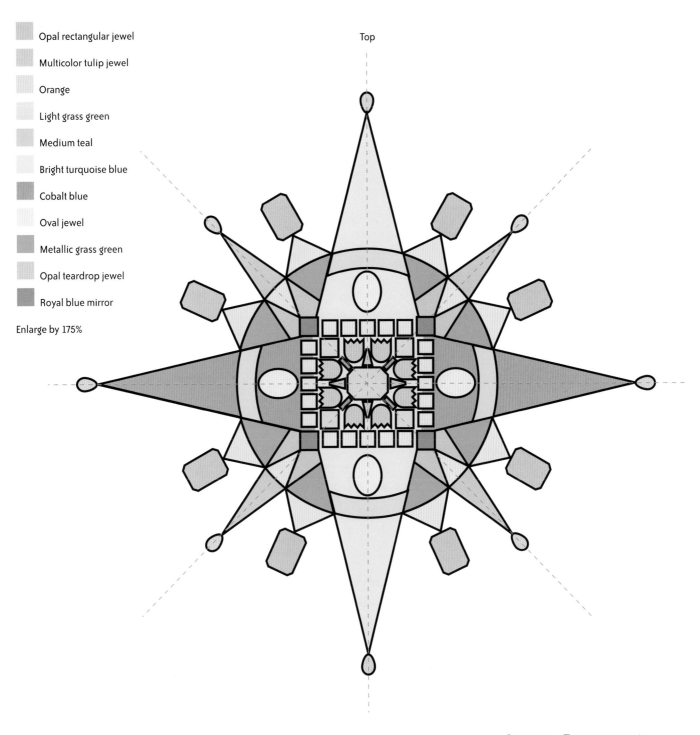

Multi-Faceted Gazing Face

(page 116)

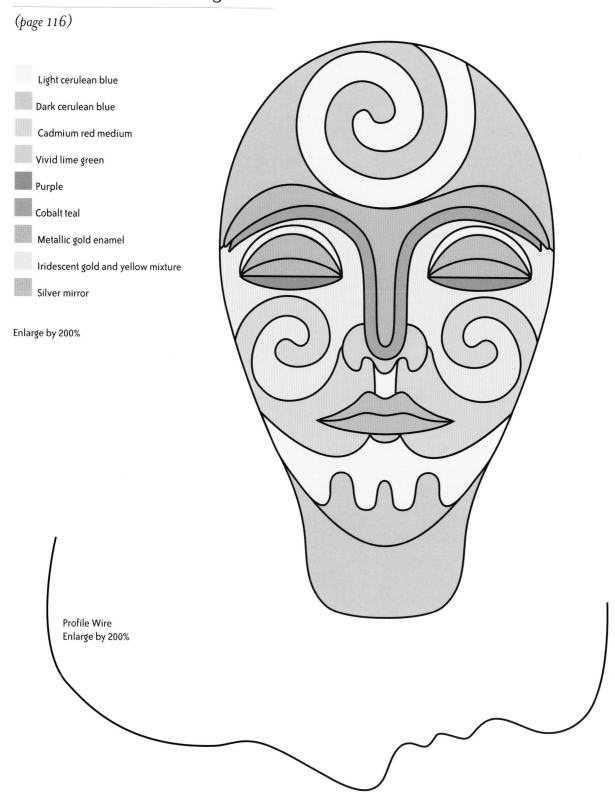

Light cerulean blue

Dark cerulean blue

Cadmium red medium

Vivid lime green

Purple

Cobalt teal

Metallic gold enamel

Iridescent gold and yellow mixture

Silver mirror

Enlarge by 200%

Profile Wire
Enlarge by 200%

Cascading Planter

(page 119)

Background Tile Pattern

Salmon

Pink

Yellow

Maroon

Enlarge by 200%
and again by 143%

Note: Grid is marked in inches; multiply
by 2.54 to convert to centimeters.

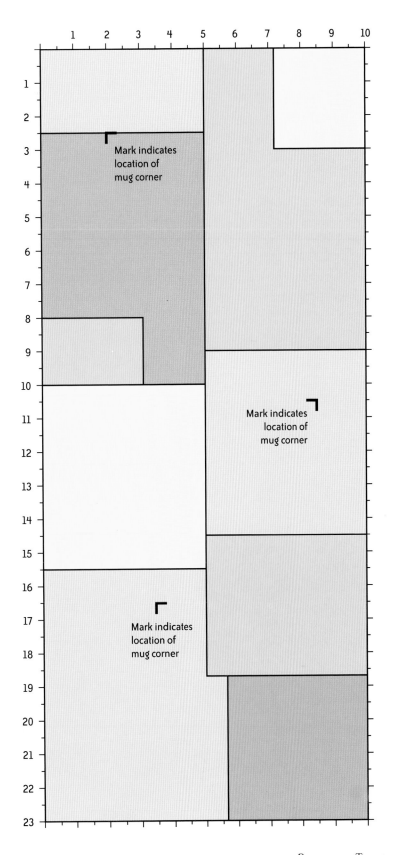

Mark indicates
location of
mug corner

Mark indicates
location of
mug corner

Mark indicates
location of
mug corner

Night and Day Flower Pot

(page 122)

- Brick red
- Medium yellow
- Metallic deep pink
- Deep red
- Sky blue
- Black
- Light olive
- Light grass-green
- Metallic deep brown
- Metallic copper

- Metallic grass-green
- Metallic baby blue
- Bright turquoise blue
- Light baby blue
- Metallic turquoise
- Light blue-green
- White

Enlarge by 200%
and again by 107%

Tape the two pieces together at the arrows.

Cheryl's Spirited Tabletop

(page 126)

Purple mirror

Rose mirror

Rust mirror

Light blue

Blue with white mix

Teal blue

Mottled green

Rust

Purple

Bright pink with
white mix

Medium pink with
white mix

Yellow

Enlarge by 160%

Dotted lines indicate edge.
Circle shapes and colors
extend over side onto
adjacent edge.

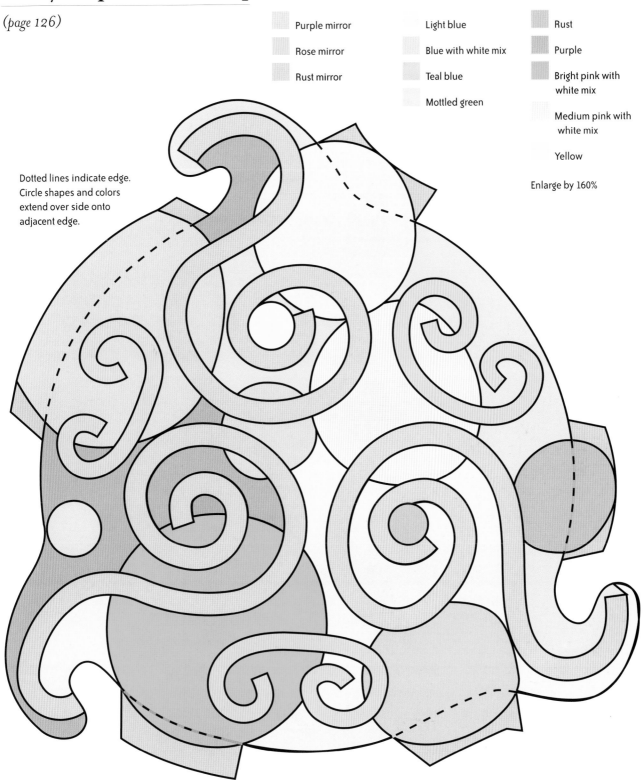

Reflecting Bird Bath/Back

(page 130)

☐ Light blue

■ Dark blue with ivory mix

☐ Light blue mirror

■ Brown

☐ Honey opal white

■ Green glass leaf jewels

■ Light and dark green
with ivory mix

■ Random combination
of iridized pale blue
and white plus teal
with white mix

■ Orange

Enlarge by 200% and
again by 109%

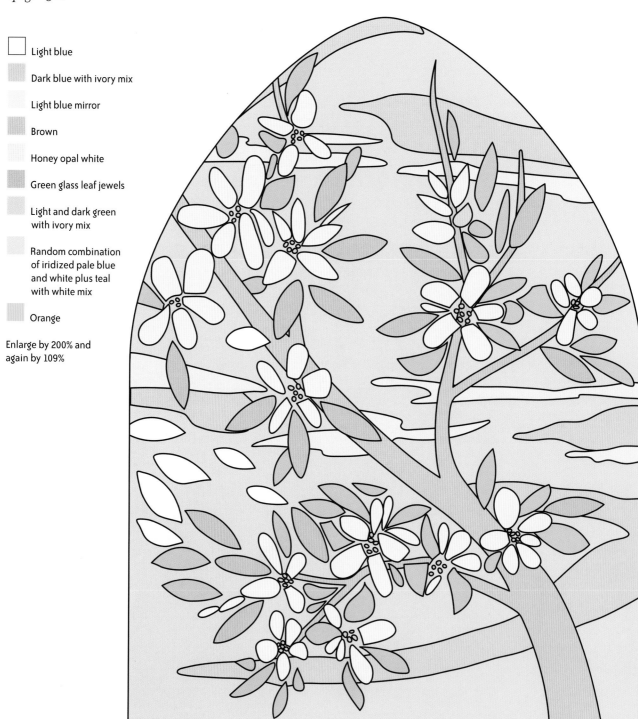

Reflecting Bird Bath/Base

(page 130)

Light blue mirror

Brown

Honey opal white

Light and dark green
with ivory mix

Random combination
of iridized pale blue
and white plus teal
with white mix

Enlarge by 200% and
again by 109%

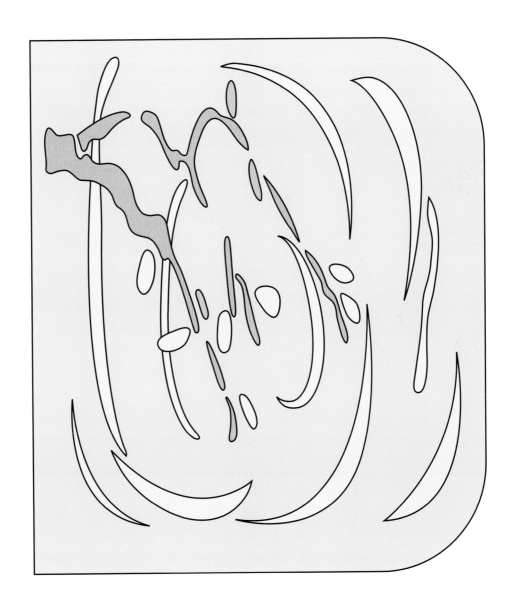

ACKNOWLEDGMENTS

Creating a book is truly a team effort. My team at Lark Books has been more than a pleasure to work with. I'd like to thank my editor, Terry Krautwurst, a consummate professional who goes the extra mile. His guidance, humor, and support were invaluable. It has been a pleasure to learn from him and I consider him not just my editor, but my friend. The same holds true for senior editor Deborah Morgenthal. This delightful, intelligent woman brought me to Lark Books, and I'm so thankful she did. All of the people at Lark have been supportive and encouraging and are very good at what they do. My thanks also go to photographer Evan Bracken and to art directors Stacey Budge and Susan McBride for making my job easier and for the book's beautiful look.

This book could not have come into existence without the support of my dear friend Craigie, whose work is featured on several pages. She and I started teaching ourselves mosaic at the same time, in the same studio. We've kept our first pieces from way back then, though we've vowed never to reveal their whereabouts! It feels wonderful to have shared this progressive and creative journey with such a generous and supportive artist friend. Craigie allowed us to photograph many of the projects in this book at her beautiful home and property, which themselves are a work of art, one always in progress.

Thank you also to Mac Buttrill for all his hard work and assistance, as well as for allowing us to use the grounds at the Watermark Bed and Breakfast in Wittman, Maryland, as the site for several project photos.

My daughter, Ashley, has been immensely helpful throughout this process by acting as head studio assistant and by actually doing portions of the mosaic work on several projects featured in this book. In fact, the Fancy Frog project on page 71 is entirely her creation. I'm thrilled that my teenager is so productive, focused, and helpful. Thanks also to my son Taylor for giving me great advice on my choice of color schemes. Though he's just 12 years old he has an uncanny eye for color and openly offers his suggestions regarding color palettes. He chose the color scheme for the Garden Shrine project on page 100, which ended up being one of my favorites.

Working with Lark Books has been a strong, healthy experience. Before we started they told me that by the end of this process I'd be glad to be rid of them. On the contrary, it has been a pleasure to collaborate with everyone at Lark. I very much appreciate this opportunity; I've learned so much.

Finally, my thanks to all the mosaic artists whose work appears and inspires throughout this book. The quality of so many different ideas and techniques is a great statement on what is possible when you have vision, imagination, and determination.

Jill MacKay

FEATURED GALLERY ARTISTS

RESOURCES

Organizations

Society for American Mosaic Artists (SAMA)
The Society of American Mosaic Artists (SAMA) is a nonprofit organization dedicated to the promotion of mosaic art and the advancement of mosaic artists through research, education, and networking. The organization's website includes links to many individual member websites.

SAMA
P.O. Box 428
Orangeburg, SC 29166
www.americanmosaics.org

Axis
Axis provides information that champions the work of contemporary artists and makers, nationally and internationally, and that stimulates opportunities for the creation, presentation and purchase of artists' work.

Axis
Leeds Metropolitan University
8 Queen Square
Leeds LS2 8AJ
West Yorkshire
United Kingdom
www.axisartists.org.uk
Tel: (+44) 0870 443 0701
Fax: (+44) 0870 443 0703
Information Service: (+44) 0870 443 0702

British Association for Modern Mosaic (BAMM)
The aim of this association is to promote, encourage and support excellence in contemporary mosaic art. Membership is open to all, including those who live outside of the United Kingdom.

BAMM
23 Lovelace Crescent
Exmouth, Devon
EX8 3PP
www.bamm.org.uk

Internet Resources

Cole Sonafrank's Internet Links to Mosaic Artists & Studios
Lists hundred of hyperlinks to other mosaic artists.
www.elvesofester.com/MosaicStudios.html

Mosaico Network
A fabulous resource with links to many mosaic-related sites, including those that showcase the work of modern masters from all over the world.
www.mosaico.net

Email Lists

There are many mosaic email discussion groups on the Internet where people share techniques, tips, and photos. Check into the available groups at any of the popular search engines.

A NOTE ABOUT SUPPLIERS

Usually, the supplies you need for making the projects in Lark books can be found at your local craft supply store, discount mart, home improvement center, or retail shop relevant to the topic of the book. Occasionally, however, you may need to buy materials or tools from specialty suppliers. In order to provide you with the most up-to-date information, we have created a list of suppliers on our Web site, which we update on a regular basis. Visit us at www.larkbooks.com, click on "Craft Supply Sources," and then click on the relevant topic. You will find numerous companies listed with their web address and/or mailing address and phone number.

INDEX